LINCOLN: His Words and His World

Bust of Lincoln by Leonard W. Volk.

LINCOLN
His Words and His World

By the Editors of COUNTRY BEAUTIFUL
Editorial Direction: Michael P. Dineen
Edited by Robert L. Polley

Published by Country Beautiful Corporation, Waukesha, Wisconsin.

President: Arthur J. Schmid Jr.

Publisher & *Editorial Director:* Michael P. Dineen

Executive Editor: Robert L. Polley

Art Director: Robert W. Pradt

Managing Editor: Dana F. Kellerman

Senior Editors: Kenneth L. Schmitz, James H. Robb

Staff: Sharon L. Griswold, Vicki Russi

CONTENTS

Now he is dead, wherefore should I fast?
Can I bring him back again? I shall go
to him, but he shall not return to me.

2 Samuel XII, 23

Wisdom crieth without; she uttereth
her voice in the streets.

Proverbs I, 20

Photograph taken by Alexander Gardner in November, 1863.

INTRODUCTION

Probably no American has been so much written about as Abraham Lincoln and seldom has any man had his life, mind and character so distorted and falsified by the romantic and sentimental nonsense of his biographers. The resulting image of a folksy, jocular backwoods saint has almost nothing to do with the facts. There is likewise little doubt that the actual Lincoln—who emerges in his own writings and conversations and in the recollections of his close personal acquaintances—was superior in deed, thought and vision to Lincoln the popular folk hero.

On the surface Lincoln usually gave the appearance of an uncomplicated man, but his personality was in many respects a puzzle and a paradox. He was, first of all, ambitious and self-confident. In 1838, when he asked: "Is it unreasonable then to expect that some man possessed of the loftiest genius, coupled with ambition sufficient to push it to its utmost stretch, will, at some time, spring up among us?" it seems probable that he saw himself in such a role. After he became President he told a friend, "You know better than any man living that from my boyhood up my ambition was to be President."

Lincoln's confidence in his superior qualities was perhaps partly based on his belief that he came from good stock. (He believed that his mother's father had been a "well-bred Virginia planter.") But, much more important, he felt that through the attributes of strong character and an active mind—honed and tested in frontier Illinois, where almost everyone began life in similar circumstances—he could and should command respect. A journalist who knew him well said: "With all [Lincoln's] awkwardness of manner and utter disregard of social conventionalities that seemed to invite familiarity, there was something about Abraham Lincoln that enforced respect." John Hay, long his private secretary, goes further: "It is absurd to call him a modest man. No great man was ever modest. It was his intellectual arrogance and unconsidered assumption of superiority that men like Salmon P. Chase* and Charles Sumner† never could forgive."

But if Lincoln was not a modest man, he was a sincerely humble and magnanimous one, humble before what he called Divine Providence and the movements of history, magnanimous in his treatment of others, the helpless (such as his pardoning of several soldiers under the death penalty) and the powerful (when asked why he didn't remove the able but controversial Secretary of War Edwin M. Stanton from office, Lincoln replied simply, "It would be difficult to find another man to fill his place"). Precisely because Lincoln had confidence in his own superior qualities he had no need to be petty nor to humiliate others. His self-confidence never became self-righteousness.

Lincoln was also a compassionate man but he kept his compassion under control so that it did not conflict with his duty as a leader to see reality clear, balanced and whole. Men, such as W. H. Herndon, Lincoln's law partner, tell us he was naturally considerate but diffident—in a way a great leader is often aloof from most people—except with his wife and children and a very few close friends. But this lack of warmth in his personal relationships did not mean that he was insensitive to the suffering of others. To the contrary, there is abundant evidence that while President his celebrated sense of humor was a means to ease the terrible burden he felt for the deaths of the war.

Two of Lincoln's other important qualities—perseverance and integrity— were recognized by almost all who knew him and can hardly be emphasized too much. Even men like Stanton, who at first lacked confidence in Lincoln, came to admire him for both his ability and his character.

About Lincoln's mind, Herndon, with perhaps some exaggeration, gives a clue: "Lincoln's perceptions were slow, cold, clear and exact. Everything came to him in its precise shape and color. . . . No lurking illusion or other error, false in itself, and clad for the moment in robes of splendor, ever passed undetected or

*Lincoln's Secretary of the Treasury.
†A leading abolitionist Senator from Massachusetts.

unchallenged over the threshold of his mind. . . . He saw all things through a perfect mental lens. There was no diffraction or refraction there."

What were the products of this mind in its maturity? Three ideas seem to be primary: He was a great admirer of the American Revolution, which he believed was "the germ which has vegetated, and still is to grow and expand into the universal liberty of mankind." He also believed that only by preserving the Union could that freedom continue to grow for the benefit of all mankind. (Another of Lincoln's convictions was that slavery is morally wrong, but he thought this principle of secondary importance to the preservation of the Union.) But all of Lincoln's ideas were cast in a frame of reference of belief in Divine Providence. This belief is best expressed in his farewell address at Springfield: "I now leave . . . with a task before me greater than that which rested upon Washington. Without the assistance of that Divine Being, who ever attended him, I cannot succeed. With that assistance I cannot fail." Thus while Lincoln was a shrewd practical politician of the first order, he always placed events in the context of their larger meaning.

And how did such a man with such a mind lead the nation through its greatest crisis? There is no easy answer to this question, but, in addition to a pervading belief in Providence, Lincoln seemed to have derived from his deep admiration for the Bible a belief in the power of the Word. Lincoln more than any other President used language as an instrument of his mind and will. He was a master at shaping language to his purpose, in persuading the popular mind and dramatizing his ideas for the American electorate. He was probably the greatest writer among American Presidents. His prose style, admired by literary critics for its excellence as well as by historians for its effectiveness, was not an accident. Again the powerful beauty of the King James version of the Bible was an influence, but as a youth Lincoln also studied books on elocution, grammar, and rhetoric that were, in some important ways, superior to many of today's school books in teaching clear, eloquent and convincing language.

Because Lincoln was the kind of man he was and because he had a remarkable understanding of and love for his country and his fellow man, his writings are much more than a political instrument or a series of literary classics. They are in fact a triumph equal in importance and meaning for us today to his act of keeping the nation whole. For his writings exhibit an admirable combination of vigor and calmness in dealing with the eternal problems of how to join equality to excellence and liberty to justice, problems still at the heart of our national concern. —ROBERT L. POLLEY

I

THE EARLY YEARS (1832-1848)

About the time the Mayflower landed at Plymouth, Massachusetts, Samuel Lincoln was born in Hingham, England. Seventeen years later he joined his older brother, Thomas, who had come to America in 1633 and was one of the six original settlers of Hingham, Massachusetts. Succeeding generations of the family migrated south and west through New Jersey and Pennsylvania until Thomas, the sixth generation of Lincolns in America, was born in Virginia in 1778. The family migrated to Kentucky where Thomas's father was killed by Indians.

In 1806 Thomas married Nancy Hanks. Their first child, Sarah, was born in 1807. Son Abraham, named for Thomas's father, was born two years later in a cabin along Nolin Creek in Hardin (now Larue) County about 40 miles south of Louisville. A third child, Thomas, died in infancy.

Thomas and his family moved to southern Indiana in 1816, the year Indiana became a state. The reason for the move, which was less than 100 miles from their Kentucky farm, was mainly because of the difficulty in obtaining clear and certain land titles in Kentucky. In Indiana Abraham attended school for a short while and received further education from his sister and read such books as the Bible, *The Adventures of Robinson Crusoe*, *Aesop's Fables*, *The Pilgrim's Progress*, Parson Weems's *Life of Washington*, *Lessons in Elocution* and *The Kentucky Preceptor*, which contained lessons for reading and speaking.

When Nancy Hanks died of a milk sickness, Abraham was 9½ and he and his sister became quite close in their grief and new dependence on each other. Fourteen months later Thomas returned to Kentucky to seek a wife and mother. He married a widow, Sarah Bush Johnston, whom Thomas and Nancy had known while living in Kentucky. Abraham was given to long periods of despondency after his sister, Sarah, died in childbirth at the age of 21. Lincoln was perhaps recalling these Indiana years when later he referred to the sadness of death scenes of loved ones.

In the spring of 1830 the Lincoln family moved to Illinois and settled on the Sangamon River a few miles west of Decatur. Abraham struck out on his own the next year and was hired to operate a store and to manage a mill in the tiny village of New Salem. He quickly gained leadership among the town's rougher elements with his physical prowess and it was here that he began his education in earnest. He studied mathematics, developed a lasting fondness for the writings of Robert Burns and Shakespeare, and joined the local debating society. He then entered politics, an obvious avenue for ambitious men on the frontier, and finished eighth out of thirteen in a race for the Legislature.

Lincoln went into debt after trying to operate a general store, mainly because of an unreliable partner, and he served as postmaster of New Salem from 1833 to 1836, did odd jobs and worked as deputy county surveyor. He ran for the Legislature in 1834 and won with bipartisan support.

While in Indiana Lincoln had read *Revised Statutes of Indiana*, lounged around the county courthouse there and had thought of becoming a lawyer as early as 1832. At the urging of a well-educated lawyer, John T. Stuart, the county's Whig leader, Lincoln began applying himself in earnest in 1834 to reading Stuart's law books whenever he found a break in his various jobs. Because of his friendship with Stuart, Lincoln was close to the state Whig leadership of the Legislature and in 1837 he was admitted to the bar. That same year he moved his residence to Springfield and set up a law practice with Stuart. Lincoln served four terms in the Legislature and during these sessions he developed into an extremely capable politician in the narrow meaning of the word, a man of expediency and limited vision.

In 1835 while Lincoln was still living in New Salem, Ann Rutledge died. Definitely established is the fact that Lincoln knew her and her family and was distressed over her death while her fiancé, a friend of Lincoln, was far away. But there is no reliable evidence that Lincoln had a romance with Ann. In 1842 in Springfield, he married Mary Todd, a vivacious, though slightly plump and somewhat emotionally immature Southern belle from Lexington, Kentucky. Although she and Lincoln came from different backgrounds and their engagement was broken once, they had several things in common, such as a love for Kentucky and an admiration for Henry Clay, whom Mary knew personally. Lincoln told her both before and after they were married that she was the only woman he had ever really loved and there is no reason to doubt the truth of that statement.

In 1841 Lincoln switched law partners and joined Stephen T. Logan, an astute and precise lawyer, and their firm became a leading one in the state. As a lawyer Lincoln was noted for his thoroughness and ability to get at the core of a controversy. In 1844 Lincoln formed a new partnership with William H. Herndon, a younger man, an association that lasted until Lincoln's death. Lincoln won election to Congress in 1846, but he was unspectacular in serving his term, although he did take an unpopular stand against President James K. Polk's Mexican War because he felt it unjust. He didn't run for re-election because of a Whig policy in the district of letting leading candidates take turns running for the office, but it is highly doubtful that he could have won. In 1849 Lincoln left active politics for five years and returned to the practice of law, growing in reputation as a lawyer and in stature as a man.

William H. Herndon, Lincoln's law partner and biographer.

Young men must not

wait to be brought forward

by the older men . . .

Communication to the People of Sangamo County, Illinois, March 9, 1832

Every man is said to have his peculiar ambition. Whether it be true or not, I can say for one that I have no other so great as that of being truly esteemed of my fellow men, by rendering myself worthy of their esteem. How far I shall succeed in gratifying this ambition, is yet to be developed. I am young and unknown to many of you. I was born and have ever remained in the most humble walks of life. I have no wealthy or popular relations to recommend me. My case is thrown exclusively upon the independent voters of this county, and if elected they will have conferred a favor upon me, for which I shall be unremitting in my labors to compensate. But if the good people in their wisdom shall see fit to keep me in the background, I have been too familiar with disappointments to be very much chagrined.

Letter to William H. Herndon, June 22, 1848

Now, as to the young men. You must not wait to be brought forward by the older men. For instance, do you suppose that I should have ever got into notice if I had waited to be hunted up and pushed forward by older men? You young men get together and form a "Rough & Ready Club" and have regular meetings and speeches. . . . Let everyone play the part he can play best—some speak, some sing and all ["holler."]

Letter to Joshua F. Speed, Feb. 25, 1842

My old father used to have a saying that "if you make a bad bargain, *hug* it the tighter"; and it occurs to me that if the bargain you have just closed [marriage] can possibly be called a bad one, it is certainly the most *pleasant one* for applying that maxim to, which my fancy can, by any effort, picture.

14

Communication to the People of Sangamo County, Illinois, March 9, 1832

That every man may receive at least a moderate education, and thereby be enabled to read the histories of his own and other countries, by which he may duly appreciate the value of our free institutions, appears to be an object of vital importance, even on this account alone, to say nothing of the advantages and satisfaction to be derived from all being able to read the Scriptures and other works both of a religious and moral nature for themselves. For my part I desire to see the time when education, and by its means, morality, sobriety, enterprise and industry, shall become much more general than at present, and should be gratified to have it in my power to contribute something to the advancement of any measure which might have a tendency to accelerate that happy period.

Letter to the Editor of the Sangamo Journal, New Salem, Illinois, June 13, 1836

I go for all sharing the privileges of the government, who assist in bearing its burthens. Consequently I go for admitting all whites to the right of suffrage, who pay taxes or bear arms, (by no means excluding females).

Address Before the Young Men's Lyceum of Springfield, Illinois, Jan. 27, 1838

. . . We, the American people . . . find ourselves in the peaceful possession, of the fairest portion of the earth, as regards extent of territory, fertility of soil and salubrity of climate. We find ourselves under the government of a system of political institutions, conducing more essentially to the ends of civil and religious liberty, than any of which the history of former times tells us. We, when mounting the stage of existence, found ourselves the legal inheritors of these fundamental blessings. We toiled not in the acquirement or establishment of them—they are a legacy bequeathed us, by a once hardy, brave, and patriotic, but now lamented and departed race of ancestors. Theirs was the task (and nobly they performed it) to possess themselves, and, through themselves, us, of this goodly land; and to uprear upon its hills and its valleys, a political edifice of liberty and equal rights; 'tis ours only, to transmit these, the former, unprofaned by the foot of an invader. . . .

At what point . . . is the approach of danger to be expected? I answer, if it ever reach us, it must spring up amongst us. . . .

Chicago Historical Society

Lincoln monument, Garfield Park, Chicago.

15

I hope I am over wary; but if I am not, there is, even now, something of ill-omen amongst us. I mean the increasing disregard for law which pervades the country; the growing disposition to substitute the wild and furious passions, in lieu of the sober judgment of courts. . . . Accounts of outrages committed by mobs form the everyday news of the times. They have pervaded the country, from New England to Louisiana; they are neither peculiar to the eternal snows of the former, nor the burning suns of the latter; they are not the creature of climate—neither are they confined to the slaveholding, or the non-slaveholding states. Alike, they spring up among the pleasure hunting masters of Southern slaves, and the order loving citizens of the land of steady habits. Whatever, then, their cause may be, it is common to the whole country.

. . . You are, perhaps, ready to ask, "What has this to do with the perpetuation of our political institutions?" I answer, it has much to do with it. Its direct consequences are, comparatively speaking, but a small evil; and much of its danger consists, in the proneness of our minds, to regard its direct as its only consequences. Abstractly considered, the hanging of the gamblers at Vicksburg was of . . . little consequence.

. . . [But] men who love tranquillity, who desire to abide by the laws, and enjoy their benefits, who would gladly spill their blood in the defense of their country; seeing their property destroyed; their families insulted; and their lives endangered; their persons injured; and seeing nothing in prospect that forebodes a change for the better; become tired of, and disgusted with, a Government that offers them no protection; and are not much averse to a change in which they imagine they have nothing to lose. Thus, then, by the operation of this mobocratic spirit, which all must admit, is now abroad in the land, the strongest bulwark of any Government, and particularly of those constituted like ours, may effectually be broken down and destroyed—I mean the attachment of the people. Whenever this effect shall be produced among us; whenever the vicious portion of population shall be permitted to gather in bands of hundreds and thousands, and burn churches, ravage and rob provision stores, throw printing presses into rivers, shoot editors and hang and burn obnoxious persons at pleasure, and with impunity; depend on it, this Government cannot last. . . .

The question recurs "how shall we fortify against it?" The answer is simple. Let every American, every lover of liberty, every well wisher to his posterity, swear by the blood of the Revolution, never to violate in the least particular, the laws of the country; and never to tolerate their violation by others.

Mary S. Owens, who turned down a marriage proposal from Lincoln.

Letter to Mary S. Owens, May 7, 1837

I am often thinking about what we said of your coming to live at Springfield. I am afraid you would not be satisfied. There is a great deal of flourishing about in carriages here, which it would be your doom to see without sharing in it. You would have to be poor without the means of hiding your poverty. Do you believe you could bear that patiently? Whatever woman may cast her lot with mine, should any ever do so, it is my intention to do all in my power to make her happy and contented; and there is nothing I can imagine, that would make me more unhappy than to fail in the effort. I know I should be much happier with you than the way I am, provided I saw no signs of discontent in you. What you have said to me may have been in jest, or I may have misunderstood it. If so, then let it be forgotten; if otherwise, I much wish you would think seriously before you decide. For my part, I have already decided. What I have said I will most positively abide by, provided you wish it. My opinion is that you had better not do it. You have not been accustomed to hardship, and it may be more severe than you now imagine. I know you are capable of thinking correctly on any subject; and if you deliberate maturely upon this, before you decide, then I am willing to abide your decision.

EDITOR'S NOTE: Lincoln and Mary Owens reached some sort of understanding in 1836 after Miss Owens came to New Salem to visit her married sister. It is evident from this letter and others (see following letter from Lincoln to Mrs. Browning) including letters from Miss Owens to W. H. Herndon, Lincoln's law partner, that both parties became dissatisfied with the prospects of the understanding.

I also tried to convince myself that the mind was much more to be valued than the person . . .

Letter to Mrs. Orville H. Browning*, April 1, 1838

Dear Madam:

Without apologizing for being egotistical, I shall make the history of so much of my own life, as has elapsed since I saw you, the subject of this letter. . . .

It was . . . in the autumn of 1836, that a married lady of my acquaintance, and who was a great friend of mine, being about to pay a visit to her father and other relatives residing in Kentucky, proposed to me, that on her return she would bring a sister of hers with her, upon condition that I would engage to become her brother-in-law with all convenient dispatch. I, of course, accepted the proposal; for you know I could not have done otherwise, had I really been averse to it; but privately between you and me, I was most confoundedly well pleased with the project. I had seen the said sister some three years before, thought her intelligent and agreeable, and saw no good objection to plodding life through hand in hand with her. Time passed on, the lady took her journey and in due time returned, sister in company sure enough. . . .

In a few days we had an interview, and although I had seen her before, she did not look as my imagination had pictured her. I knew she was over-size, but she now appeared a fair match for Falstaff; I knew she was called an "old maid," and I felt no doubt of the truth of at least half of the appellation; but now, when I beheld her, I could not for my life avoid

*The political careers of Lincoln and Orville Browning of Quincy, Illinois began only two years apart and they remained closely associated throughout Lincoln's life. Socially, Mrs. Browning was one of Lincoln's most valued friends.

thinking of my mother; and this, not from withered features, for her skin was too full of fat, to permit its contracting into wrinkles; but from her want of teeth, weather-beaten appearance in general, and from a kind of notion that ran in my head, that nothing could have commenced at the size of infancy, and reached her present bulk in less than thirty-five or forty years; and, in short, I was not all pleased with her. But what could I do? I had told her sister that I would take her for better or for worse; and I made a point of honor and conscience in all things, to stick to my word, especially if others had been induced to act on it, which in this case, I doubted not they had, for I was now fairly convinced, that no other man on earth would have her, and hence the conclusion that they were bent on holding me to my bargain. Well, thought I, I have said it, and be consequences what they may, it shall not be my fault if I fail to do it. At once I determined to consider her my wife; and this done, all my powers of discovery were put to the rack, in search of perfections in her, which might be fairly set-off against her defects. I tried to imagine she was handsome, which, but for her unfortunate corpulency, was actually true. Exclusive of this, no woman that I have seen has a finer face. I also tried to convince myself, that the mind was much more to be valued than the person; and in this, she was not inferior, as I could discover, to any with whom I had been acquainted.

Shortly after this, without attempting to come to any positive understanding with her, I set out for Vandalia, where and when you first saw me. During

What a noble ally this,

to the cause of political freedom . . .

my stay there, I had letters from her, which did not change my opinion of either her intellect or intention; but on the contrary, confirmed it in both. . . .

After my return home, I saw nothing to change my opinion of her in any particular. She was the same and so was I. . . .

After all my suffering upon this deeply interesting subject, here I am, wholly unexpectedly, completely out of the "scrape" . . . out clear in every sense of the term; no violation of word, honor or conscience. . . .

After I had delayed the matter as long as I thought I could in honor do, which by the way had brought me round into the last fall, I concluded I might as well bring it to a consummation without further delay; and so I mustered my resolution, and made the proposal to her direct; but, shocking to relate, she answered, No. At first I supposed she did it through an affection of modesty, which I thought but ill-become her, under the peculiar circumstances of her case; but on my renewal of the charge, I found she repelled it with greater firmness than before. I tried it again and again, but with the same success, or rather with the same want of success. I finally was forced to give it up, at which I very unexpectedly found myself mortified almost beyond endurance. I was mortified, it seemed to me, in a hundred different ways. My vanity was deeply wounded by the reflection, that I had so long been too stupid to discover her intentions, and at the same time never doubting that I understood them perfectly; and also, that she whom I had taught myself to believe no body else would have, had actually rejected me with all my fancied greatness; and to cap the whole, I then, for the first time, began to suspect that I was really a little in love with her. But let it all go. I'll try and out live it. Others have been made fools of by the girls; but this can never be with truth said of me. I most emphatically, in this instance, made a fool of myself. I have now come to the conclusion never again to think of marrying; and for this reason; I can never be satisfied with any one who would be block-head enough to have me.

Temperance Address, Springfield, Illinois, Feb. 22, 1842

In my judgment, such of us as have never fallen victims [of intemperance] have been spared more by the absence of appetite than from any mental or moral superiority over those who have. Indeed, I believe if we take habitual drunkards as a class, their heads and hearts will bear an advantageous comparison with those of any other class. There seems ever to have been a proneness in the brilliant and the warm-blooded to fall into this vice. The demon of intemperance ever seems to have delighted in sucking the blood of genius and of generosity. . . .

Turn now, to the temperance revolution. In it, we shall find a stronger bondage broken; a viler slavery manumitted; a greater tyrant deposed. In it, more of want supplied, more disease healed, more sorrow assuaged. By it no orphans starving, no widows weeping. By it, none wounded in feeling, none injured in interest. Even the dram-maker, and dram seller, will have glided into other occupations so gradually, as never to have felt the shock of change; and will stand ready to join all others in the universal song of gladness.

And what a noble ally this, to the cause of political freedom. With such an aid, its march cannot fail to be on and on, till every son of earth shall drink in rich fruition, the sorrow quenching draughts of perfect liberty. Happy day, when, all appetites controlled, all passions subdued, all matters subjected, mind, all conquering mind, shall live and move the monarch of the world. Glorious consummation! Hail fall of Fury! Reign of Reason, all hail!

And when the victory shall be complete—when there shall be neither a slave nor a drunkard on the earth—how proud the title of that land, which may truly claim to be the birthplace and the cradle of both those revolutions, that shall have ended in that victory. How nobly distinguished that people, who shall have planted, and nurtured to maturity, both the political and moral freedom of their species.

This is the 110th anniversary of the birthday of Washington. We are met to celebrate this day. Washington is the mightiest name of earth—long since mightiest in the cause of civil liberty; still mightiest in moral reformation. On that name, an eulogy is expected. It cannot be. To add brightness to the sun, or glory to the name of Washington, is alike impossible. Let none attempt it. In solemn awe pronounce the name, and in its naked deathless splendor, leave it shining on.

HOME OF ABRAHAM LINCOLN.

Lincoln's Springfield home as depicted in a print that appeared between 1861 and 1865.

Indians in Kentucky killing Lincoln's grandfather, also named Abraham, as imagined by an artist many decades after the event.

Mary Todd Lincoln in Springfield four years after her marriage.

Handbill Replying to Charges of Infidelity, July 31, 1846

FELLOW CITIZENS:

A charge having got into circulation in some of the neighborhoods of this District, in substance that I am an open scoffer at Christianity, I have by the advice of some friends concluded to notice the subject in this form. That I am not a member of any Christian church is true; but I have never denied the truth of the Scriptures; and I have never spoken with intentional disrespect of religion in general, or of any denomination of Christians in particular. It is true that in early life I was inclined to believe in what I understand is called the "Doctrine of Necessity"—that is, that the human mind is impelled to action, or held in rest by some power, over which the mind itself has no control; and I have sometimes (with one, two or three, but never publicly) tried to maintain this opinion in argument. The habit of arguing thus however, I have entirely left off for more than five years. And I add here, I have always understood this same opinion to be held by several of the Christian denominations. The foregoing, is the whole truth, briefly stated, in relation to myself, upon this subject.

I do not think I could myself, be brought to support a man for office, whom I knew to be an open enemy of, and scoffer at, religion. Leaving the higher matter of eternal consequences between him and his Maker, I still do not think any man has the right thus to insult the feelings, and injure the morals, of the community in which he may live. If, then, I was guilty of such conduct, I should blame no man who should condemn me for it; but I do blame those, whoever they may be, who falsely put such a charge in circulation against me.

Fragment: Notes for a Law Lecture, July 1, 1850?

I am not an accomplished lawyer. I find quite as much material for a lecture in those points wherein I have failed, as in those wherein I have been moderately successful. The leading rule for the lawyer, as for the man of every other calling, is diligence. Leave nothing for tomorrow which can be done today. Never let your correspondence fall behind. Whatever piece of business you have in hand, before stopping, do all the labor pertaining to it which can then be done. When you bring a common-law suit, if you have the facts for doing so, write the declaration at once. . . . Extemporaneous speaking should be practiced and cultivated. It is the lawyer's avenue to the public. However able and faithful he may be in other respects, people are slow to bring him business if he cannot make a speech. And yet there is not a more fatal error to young lawyers than relying too much on speech-making. If any one, upon his rare powers of speaking, shall claim an exemption from the drudgery of the law, his case is a failure in advance.

Discourage litigation. Persuade your neighbors to compromise whenever you can. Point out to them how the nominal winner is often a real loser—in fees, expenses and waste of time. As a peacemaker the lawyer has a superior opportunity of being a good man. There will still be business enough.

Never stir up litigation. A worse man can scarcely be found than one who does this.

Fragments of a Tariff Discussion, Dec. 1, 1847?

In the early days of the world, the Almighty said to the first of our race, "In the sweat of thy face shalt thou eat bread"; and since then, if we expect the light and the air of heaven, no good thing has been, or can be enjoyed by us, without having first cost labor. And, inasmuch [as] most good things are produced by labor, it follows that [all] such things of right belong to those whose labor has produced them. But it has so happened in all ages of the world, that some have labored, and others have, without labor, enjoyed a large proportion of the fruits. This is wrong, and should not continue. To [secure] to each laborer the whole product of his labor, or as nearly as possible, is a most worthy object of any good government. But then the question arises, how can a government best effect this? In our own country, in its present condition, will the protective principle advance or retard this object? Upon this subject, the habits of our whole species fall into three great classes—useful labor, useless labor and idleness. Of these the first only is meritorious; and to it all the products of labor rightfully belong; but the two latter, while they exist, are heavy pensioners upon the first, robbing it of a large portion of its just rights. The only remedy for this is to, as far as possible, drive useless labor and idleness out of existence.

Speech in U.S. House of Representatives on Internal Improvements, Washington, D.C., June 20, 1848

I wish now to submit a few remarks on the general proposition of amending the Constitution. As a general rule, I think we would [do] much better [to] let it alone. No slight occasion should tempt us to touch it. Better not take the first step, which may lead to a habit of altering it. Better, rather, habituate ourselves to think of it as unalterable. It can scarcely be made better than it is. New provisions would introduce new difficulties, and thus create an increased appetite for still further change. No sir, let it stand as it is. New hands have never touched it. The men who made it have done their work and have passed away. Who shall improve on what *they* did?

Nothing can be enjoyed

by us without it first

having cost labor . . .

An artist's conception of Lincoln studying by the fire while living in Indiana.

Lincoln addressing the court in Shelbyville, Illinois, 1856.

Speech in U.S. House of Representatives on the Presidential Question, Washington, D.C., July 27, 1848

But I suppose I can not reasonably hope to convince you that we have any principles. The most I can expect, is to assure you that we think we have, and are quite contented with them. The other day, one of the gentlemen from Georgia (Mr. Iverson) an eloquent man, and a man of learning, so far as I could judge, not being learned, myself, came down upon us astonishingly. He spoke in what the Baltimore American calls the "scathing and withering style." At the end of his second severe flash, I was struck blind, and found myself feeling with my fingers for an assurance of my continued physical existence. A little of the bone was left, and I gradually revived. He eulogized Mr. Clay in high and beautiful terms, and then declared that we had deserted all our principles, and had turned Henry Clay out, like an old horse, to root. This is terribly severe. It can not be answered by argument; at least, I can not so answer it. I merely wish to ask the gentleman if the Whigs are the only party he can think of, who some times turn old horses out to root. Is not a certain Martin Van Buren, an old horse which your own party have turned out to root and is he not rooting a little to your discomfort about now? . . .

But the gentleman [Alfred Iverson] from Georgia further says we have deserted all our principles, and taken shelter under General Taylor's military coat-tail; and he seems to think this is exceedingly degrading. Well, as his faith is, so be it unto him. But can he remember no other military coat-tail under which a certain other party have been sheltering for near a quarter of a century? Has he no acquaintance with the ample military coat-tail of General Jackson? Does he not know that his own party have run the five last Presidential races under that coat-tail? and that they are now running the sixth, under the same cover? Yes sir, that coat-tail was used, not only for General Jackson himself; but has been clung to, with the gripe of death, by every democratic candidate since. You have never ventured, and dare not now venture, from under it. Your campaign papers have constantly been "Old Hickories" with rude likenesses of the old general upon them; hickory poles, and hickory brooms, your never-ending emblems; Mr. Polk himself was "Young Hickory," "Little Hickory" or something so; and even now, your campaign paper here, is proclaiming that Cass and Butler are of the true "Hickory stripe." No sir, you dare not give it up.

Like a horde of hungry ticks you have stuck to the tail of the Hermitage lion to the end of his life; and you are still sticking to it, and drawing a loathsome sustenance from it, after he is dead. A fellow once advertised that he had made a discovery by which he could make a new man out of an old one, and have enough of the stuff left to make a little yellow dog. Just such a discovery has General Jackson's popularity been to you. You not only twice made President of him out of it, but you have had enough of the stuff left, to make Presidents of several comparatively small men since; and it is your chief reliance now to make still another.

As a peacemaker the lawyer has a superior opportunity of being

a good man. There will still be business enough . . .

Shirley Althoff & Dick Weddle

An original structure at New Salem, Illinois, is the cooperage where Lincoln is said to have done some of his studying.

I suppose I cannot hope to convince you that we have any principles.

The two oil portraits, above and on the facing page, are by the same artist, George F. Wright.

The most I can expect is to assure you that we think we have . . .

Lincoln had always been clean shaven until he began to let his beard grow in the fall of 1860.

II

THE LINCOLN-DOUGLAS DEBATES

Lincoln first met Stephen A. Douglas when Lincoln went to Vandalia in 1834, to attend his first session of the Legislature. Douglas, four years younger than Lincoln, was about 5 feet 4 inches tall, sturdily built, with piercing eyes, a resonant voice and alert manner.

In the Congressional session of 1852–1853 while Lincoln was in political retirement, Senator Douglas, as chairman of the powerful Committee on Territories, guided through Congress the Kansas-Nebraska Bill which provided that the question of slavery in each territory be decided by "popular sovereignty," a fundamental principle with Douglas. It was this controversy which Lincoln took as a moral challenge and which reawakened his interest in politics, at first without thought to a new political career for himself. Lincoln's view that slavery was morally wrong put the slavery question for him beyond the realm of popular sovereignty. Douglas, on the other hand, lacked any moral sensitiveness about slavery and did not comprehend the depth of Northern feeling on the subject.

The Kansas-Nebraska Act snapped frayed party lines and by 1856 Lincoln identified himself as a Republican, receiving some support for the Republican Vice-Presidential nomination that year. In 1858 he ran as a Republican against Douglas for the Senate and, at the beginning of the campaign, he followed Douglas around from town to town because the more famous Senator would draw large crowds to which Lincoln would speak later. Partly to escape the ridicule of the Douglas press for this maneuver, Lincoln challenged Douglas to a series of debates. Douglas had nothing to gain but he accepted. During the series, which drew excited crowds of from 10,000 to 15,000 for each debate, Lincoln was at first on the defensive, but he gradually began to improve his position by stressing the moral issue.

The Republican candidates for the Legislature—which elected Senators in those days—received more votes than the Democrats but outdated apportionment gave victory to the Democrats and Douglas.

The primary results of the debates were that Lincoln, under Douglas's sharp attacks, formulated his thoughts more clearly and he had become a national figure known for his moderate position without at the same time antagonizing the abolitionists.

Lincoln and Douglas were opponents for most of their political careers. Two years after their famous debates they were, as shown by these cartoons of 1860, among the four major candidates for President. Above: "Uncle Sam Making New Arrangements." Below: "Lincoln Shows Douglas the Right Road to the White House."

Destroy the spirit of liberty

and you have planted

the seeds of despotism . . .

Stephen A. Douglas, "The Little Giant."

Speech, Springfield, Illinois, July 17, 1858

. . . Nobody has ever expected me to be President. In my poor, lean, lank face nobody has ever seen that any cabbages were sprouting out.

Fifth Debate, Galesburg, Illinois, Oct. 7, 1858

. . . While Mr. Jefferson was the owner of slaves, as undoubtedly he was, in speaking upon this very subject, he used the strong language that "he trembled for his country when he remembered that God was just . . . ."

Speech, Edwardsville, Illinois, Sept. 11, 1858

. . . When . . . you have succeeded in dehumanizing the Negro; when you have put him down and made it forever impossible for him to be but as the beasts of the field; when you have extinguished his soul and placed him where the ray of hope is blown out in darkness . . . of the damned, are you quite sure that the demon which you have roused *will not turn and rend you?* What constitutes the bulwark of our own liberty and independence? It is not our frowning battlements, our bristling sea coasts, the guns of our war steamers, or the strength of our gallant and disciplined army. These are not our reliance against a resumption of tyranny in our fair land. All of them may be turned against our liberties without making us stronger or weaker for the struggle. Our reliance is in the *love of liberty* which God has planted in our bosoms. Our defense is in the preservation of the spirit which prizes liberty as the heritage of all men, in all lands everywhere. Destroy this spirit, and you have planted the seeds of despotism around your own doors. Familiarize yourselves with the chains of bondage and you are preparing your own limbs to wear them. Accustomed to trample on the rights of those around you, you have lost the genius of your own independence and become the fit subjects of the first cunning tyrant who rises.

Seventh Debate, Alton, Illinois, Oct. 15, 1858

. . . When this new principle [that the Declaration of Independence does not include the Negro]—this new proposition that no human being ever thought of three years ago—is brought forward, *I combat it* as having an evil tendency, if not an evil design; I combat it as having a tendency to dehumanize the Negro —to take away from him the right of ever striving to be a man. I combat it as being one of the thousand things constantly done in these days to prepare the public mind to make property, and nothing but property, of the *Negro in all the states of this Union.*

Lincoln the liberator of the slaves, Lincoln Park, Washington, D.

MANCIPATION

. . . Mr. [Henry] Clay . . . said that "those who would repress all tendencies to liberty and ultimate emancipation [of slaves] must . . . go back to the era of our liberty and independence, and muzzle the cannon that thunders its annual joyous return—they must blot out the moral lights around us—they must penetrate the human soul, and eradicate the light of reason and the love of liberty." And I do think . . . that Judge Douglas, and whoever like him teaches that the Negro has no share, humble though it may be, in the Declaration of Independence, is going back to the era of our liberty and independence, and, so far as in him lies, muzzling the cannon that thunders its annual joyous return; that he is blowing out the moral lights around us, when he contends that whoever wants slaves has a right to hold them; that he is penetrating, so far as lies in his power, the human soul, and eradicating the light of reason and the love of liberty, when he is in every possible way preparing the public mind, by his vast influence, for making the institution of slavery perpetual and national.

The first inference seems to be that if you do not enslave the Negro, you are wronging the white man in some way or other; and that whoever is opposed to the Negro being enslaved is in some way or other against the white man. Is not that a falsehood? If there was a necessary conflict between the white man and the Negro, I should be for the white man as much as Judge Douglas; but I say there is no such necessary conflict. I say that there is room enough for us all to be free. . . .

That is the issue that will continue in this country when these poor tongues of Judge Douglas and myself shall be silent. It is the eternal struggle between these two principles—right and wrong—throughout the world. They are the two principles that have stood face to face from the beginning of time; and will ever continue to struggle. The one is the common right of humanity and the other the divine right of kings. It is the same principle in whatever shape it develops itself. It is the same spirit that says, "You toil and work and earn bread, and I'll eat it." No matter in what shape it comes, whether from the mouth of a king who seeks to bestride the people of his own nation and live by the fruit of their labor, or from one race of men as an apology for enslaving another race, it is the same tyrannical principle.

In the course of my main argument, Judge Douglas interrupted me to say, that the principle [of] the Nebraska bill was very old; that it originated when God made man and placed good and evil before him, allowing him to choose for himself, being responsible for the choice he should make. At the time I thought this was merely playful; and I answered it accordingly. But in his reply to me he renewed it, as a serious argument. In seriousness then, the facts of this proposition are not true as stated. God did not place good and evil before man, telling him to make his choice. On the contrary, he did tell him there was one tree, of the fruit of which he should not eat, upon pain of certain death. I should scarcely wish so strong a prohibition against slavery in Nebraska.

But this argument strikes me as not a little remarkable in another particular—in its strong resemblance to the old argument for the "divine right of kings." By the latter, the king is to do just as he pleases with his white subjects, being responsible to God alone. By the former the white man is to do just as he pleases with his black slaves, being responsible to God alone. The two things are precisely alike; and it is but natural that they should find similar arguments to sustain them.

I protest, now and forever, against that counterfeit logic which presumes that because I do not want a Negro woman for a slave, I do necessarily want her for a wife. My understanding is that I need not have her for either, but, as God has made us separate, we can leave one another alone, and do one another much good thereby.

All I ask for the Negro is that if you do not like him, let him alone. If God gave him but little, that little let him enjoy.

. . . I confess myself as belonging to that class in the country who contemplate slavery as a moral, social and political evil, having due regard for its actual existence amongst us and the difficulties of getting rid of it in any satisfactory way, and to all the constitutional obligations which have been thrown about it; but, nevertheless, desire a policy that looks to the prevention of it as a wrong, and looks hopefully to the time when as a wrong it may come to an end.

Sixth Debate, Quincy, Illinois, Oct. 13, 1858

. . . The leading man—I think I may do my friend Judge Douglas the honor of calling him such—advocating the present Democratic policy, never himself says it [slavery] is wrong. He has the high distinction, so far as I know, of never having said slavery is either right or wrong. Almost everybody says one or the other, but the judge never does.

Fifth Debate, Galesburg, Illinois, Oct. 7, 1858

Judge Douglas declares that if any community want slavery they have a right to have it. He can say that logically, if he says that there is no wrong in slavery; but if you admit that there is a wrong in it, he cannot logically say that anybody has a right to do wrong.

Speech, Springfield, Illinois, June 26, 1857

If the people of Utah shall peacefully form a state constitution tolerating polygamy, will the Democracy admit them into the Union?" There is nothing in the United States Constitution or law against polygamy; and why is it not a part of the judge's [Douglas] "sacred right of self-government" for that people to have it, or rather to *keep* it, if they choose?

Speech, Springfield, Illinois, June 16, 1858

In *my* opinion, it [slavery] *will* not cease until a *crisis* shall have been reached and passed.

Fourth Debate, Charleston, Illinois, Sept. 18, 1858

. . . There is a physical difference between the white and black races which, I believe, will forever forbid the two races living together on terms of social and political equality. And inasmuch as they cannot so live, while they do remain together there must be the position of superior and inferior, and I, as much as any other man, am in favor of having the superior position assigned to the white race. . . . I do not perceive that because the white man is to have the superior position the Negro should be denied everything.

Speech, Chicago, Illinois, July 10, 1858

. . . Let us discard all this quibbling about this man and the other man—this race and that race and the other race being inferior, and therefore they must be placed in an inferior position. . . . Let us discard all these things, and unite as one people throughout this land, until we shall once more stand up declaring that all men are created equal.

Lincoln speaking during one of the debates with Douglas, who is at Lincoln's immediate right.

III

LINCOLN AND THE NEGROES

During the debates of 1858, Senator Douglas belabored Lincoln on the question of the equality of Negroes until the sorely pressed Lincoln stated, as he had before, that he believed physical differences between the races would "forever forbid the two races living together on terms of social and political equality." Douglas said this hardly squared with what Lincoln had said once before: "Let us discard all this quibbling about . . . this race and that race . . . being inferior . . . and unite as one people . . . until we shall once more stand up declaring that all men are equal."

Actually Lincoln believed both statements to be true. He did regard the Negro race as inferior but this did not mean that the Negro was to be deprived of his American heritage of equal opportunity. Lincoln did not believe that a man's rights were contingent upon his abilities. In fact Lincoln was partially to change his view about the Negro's political rights; in 1864 Lincoln made what was perhaps the earliest proposition from any official source to grant suffrage to the Negro.

"Growth" is the best word to describe Lincoln's attitudes toward the Negro. Even Lincoln's hatred of slavery was no sudden conversion. In Kentucky his parents attended a Baptist church that opposed slavery during a time of great controversy in the area about the subject. During two trips to New Orleans, the center for the sale of slaves, he probably saw a slave auction, in addition to the sight he recounts in his letter to Joshua Speed (page 34). As a result, he came to the unwavering belief that slavery was morally wrong, that it was economically harmful to white workers who had to compete with unpaid labor, that it endangered democracy because it went against the principle that governments derive their powers from the consent of the governed, and that it opposed the Declaration of Independence to which Lincoln was devoted.

In the Presidency he continued to grow in his understanding of the Negro and his problems, although he only reluctantly gave up his plan for Negro colonization and he never apparently sensed that without social equality the Negro could never enjoy full equality of opportunity; but he genuinely disliked speaking of any so-called inequality between races. This growth can be demonstrated by his change from a belief in gradual emancipation to full support for the 13th Amendment of 1865 which ended slavery in all states and territories, a much more comprehensive and authoritative document than the earlier Emancipation Proclamation which was conceived primarily as a military and diplomatic maneuver to disrupt the South and to emphasize the moral character of the Civil War.

But the real measure of Lincoln and the Negro was the Negro's attitude toward him. Although Lincoln's views of the Negro were not without imperfections, he was far ahead of most of his fellow white Americans of the time. The Negro sensed this and something more, a basic love and humanity to a degree that is in few men. The Negro loved Lincoln first and longest and possesses him like no other American. The Negro's feeling about Lincoln has many roots and takes many forms—hero worship, father figure, messianic deliverer—but whatever its basis it convinced them, for the first time, that they had a stake in America. This feeling was perhaps best expressed by a former slave at Chapel Hill, North Carolina, after Lincoln's assassination:

> He is gone out of glory to glory,
> A smile with the tear may be shed.
> Oh, then let us tell the sweet story—
> Triumphantly, Lincoln is dead.

A Southern slave auction, the existence of which violently stirred Northern emotions.

Lincoln statue by Haig Patigan, San Francisco City Hall.

board, ten or a dozen slaves, shackled together with irons. That sight was continual torment to me; and I see something like it every time I touch the Ohio, or any other slave-border. It is hardly fair for you to assume, that I have no interest in a thing which has, and continually exercises, the power of making me miserable. You ought rather to appreciate how much the great body of the Northern people do crucify their feelings, in order to maintain their loyalty to the Constitution and the Union.

Fragment on Pro-Slavery Theology, Oct. 1, 1858?

Suppose it is true that the Negro is inferior to the white in the gifts of nature; is it not the exact reverse of justice that the white should for that reason take from the Negro any part of the little which has been given him. "*Give* to him that is needy" is the Christian rule of charity; but "Take from him that is needy" is the rule of slavery.

No man ever got closer to Lincoln than Joshua F. Speed. When Lincoln first went to Springfield in 1837 he shared a room with Speed over the latter's store.

Letter to Joshua F. Speed, Aug. 24, 1855

You suggest that in political action now, you and I would differ. I suppose we would; not quite as much, however, as you may think. You know I dislike slavery and you fully admit the abstract wrong of it. So far there is no cause of difference. But you say that sooner than yield your legal right to the slave—especially at the bidding of those who are not themselves interested, you would see the Union dissolved. I am not aware that *any one* is bidding you to yield that right; very certainly *I* am not. I leave that matter entirely to yourself. I also acknowledge *your* rights and *my* obligations, under the Constitution, in regard to your slaves. I confess I hate to see the poor creatures hunted down, and caught, and carried back to their stripes, and unrewarded toils; but I bite my lip and keep quiet. In 1841 you and I had together a tedious low-water trip, on a steamboat from Louisville to St. Louis. You may remember, as I well do, that from Louisville to the mouth of the Ohio there were, on

Our government began by affirming the equal rights of men . . .

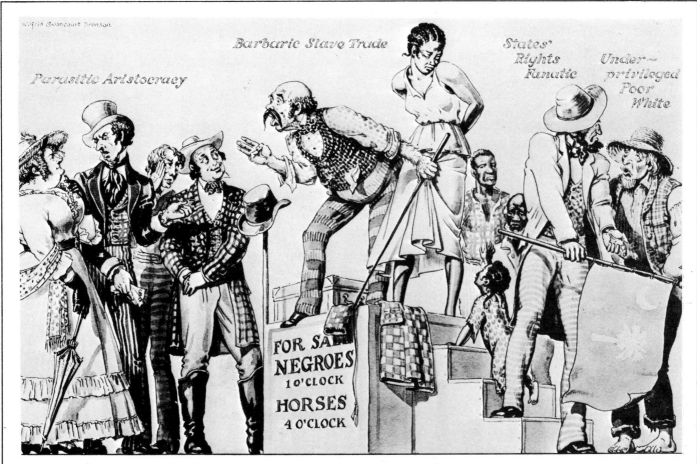

A Northern cartoon revealing the way the North felt about the South.

Speech, New Haven, Connecticut, March 6, 1860

When men are framing a supreme law and chart of government to secure blessings and prosperity to untold generations yet to come, they use language as short and direct and plain as can be found to express their meaning. In all matters but this of slavery the framers of the Constitution used the very clearest, shortest and most direct language. But the Constitution alludes to slavery three times without mentioning it once! The language used becomes ambiguous, roundabout and mystical. . . . We cannot doubt that it was done on purpose. Only one reason is possible, and that is supplied us by one of the framers of the Constitution—and it is not possible for men to conceive of any other—they expected and desired that the system would come to an end, and meant that when it did the Constitution should not show that there ever had been a slave in this good free country of ours!

Speech, Springfield, Illinois, June 26, 1857

I think the authors of that notable instrument [the Declaration of Independence] intended to include *all* men, but they did not intend to declare all men

35

equal *in all respects*. They did not mean to say all were equal in color, size, intellect, moral developments or social capacity. They defined with tolerable distinctness in what respects they did consider all men created equal—equal in "certain inalienable rights, among which are life, liberty and the pursuit of happiness." This they said, and this they meant. They did not mean to assert the obvious untruth that all were then actually enjoying that equality, nor yet that they were about to confer it immediately upon them. In fact, they had no power to confer such a boon. They meant simply to declare the *right*; so that the *enforcement* of it might follow as fast as circumstances should permit.

Fragment on Slavery, July 1, 1854?

Most governments have been based, practically, on the denial of equal rights of men. . . . Ours began by affirming those rights. They said, some men are too ignorant and vicious to share in government. Possibly so, said we; and, by your system, you would always keep them ignorant and vicious. We proposed to give all a chance; and we expected the weak to grow stronger, the ignorant wiser and all better and happier together. We made the experiment, and the fruit is before us. . . . Look at it in its aggregate grandeur. . . .

Letter to Joshua F. Speed, Aug. 24, 1855

Our progress in degeneracy appears to me to be pretty rapid. As a nation, we began by declaring that "*all men are created equal.*" We now practically read it "all men are created equal, *except Negroes.*" When the Know-Nothings get control, it will read "all men are created equal, except Negroes, *and foreigners, and Catholics.*" When it comes to this I should prefer emigrating to some country where they make no pretence of loving liberty—to Russia, for instance, where despotism can be taken pure, and without the base alloy of hypocrisy.

Speech, Lewistown, Illinois, Aug. 7, 1858

Wise statesmen as they [authors of the Declaration of Independence] were, they knew the tendency of prosperity to breed tyrants, and so they established these great self-evident truths, that when in the distant future some man, some faction, some interest, should set up the doctrine that none but rich men, or none but white men, were entitled to life, liberty and the pursuit of happiness, their posterity might look up again to the Declaration of Independence and take courage to renew the battle which their fathers began. . . .

Speech at Sanitary Fair, Baltimore, Maryland, April 18, 1864

The world has never had a good definition of the word "liberty," and the American people, just now, are much in want of one. We all declare for liberty; but in using the same *word* we do not all mean the same *thing*. With some the word "liberty" may mean for each man to do as he pleases with himself, and the product of his labor; while with others the same word may mean for some men to do as they please with other men, and the product of other men's labor. Here are two, not only different, but incompatible things, called by the same name—"liberty." And it follows that each of the things is, by the respective parties, called by two different and incompatible names—"liberty" and "tyranny."

Letter to George Robertson, Aug. 15, 1855

When we were the political slaves of King George, and wanted to be free, we called the maxim that "all men are created equal" a self-evident truth, but now when we have grown fat, and have lost all dread of being slaves ourselves, we have become so greedy to be *masters* that we call the same maxim "a self-evident lie."

Speech, Cincinnati, Ohio, Sept. 17, 1859

When we do as we say, beat you [proslavery advocates], you perhaps want to know what we will do with you. . . . We mean to treat you, as near as we possibly can, like Washington, Jefferson and Madison treated you. We mean to leave you alone, and in no way to interfere with your institution [slavery]; to abide by all and every compromise of the Constitution. . . . We mean to remember that you are as good as we; that there is no difference between us other than the difference of circumstances. We mean to recognize and bear in mind always that you have as good hearts in your bosoms as other people, or as we claim to have, and treat you accordingly. We marry your girls when we have a chance—the white ones, I mean—and I have the honor to inform you that I once did have a chance in that way.

Speech, Kalamazoo, Michigan, Aug. 27, 1856

. . . Southern newspapers . . . insist that slavery has a right to spread. They defend it upon principle. They insist that their slaves are far better off than Northern freemen. What a mistaken view do these men have of Northern laborers! They think that men are always to remain laborers here—but there is no such class.

Speech, Peoria, Illinois, Oct. 16, 1854

. . . I think I have no prejudice against the Southern people. They are just what we would be in their situation. If slavery did not now exist amongst them, they would not introduce it. If it did now exist amongst us, we should not instantly give it up. . . . We know that some Southern men do free their slaves, go north and become tip-top abolitionists, while some Northern ones go south and become most cruel slave-masters.

Speech, Peoria, Illinois, Oct. 16, 1854

When it is said that the institution [slavery] exists, and that it is very difficult to get rid of it in any satisfactory way, I can understand and appreciate the saying. I surely will not blame them [men of the South] for not doing what I should not know how to do myself. If all earthly power were given me, I should not know what to do as to the existing institution. My first impulse would be to free all the slaves and send them to Liberia, to their own native land. But a moment's reflection would convince me that whatever of high hope—as I think there is—there may be in this, in the long run, its sudden execution is impossible. If they were all landed there in a day, they would all perish in the next ten days; and there are not surplus shipping and surplus money enough in the world to carry them there in many times ten days.

Speech, Peoria, Illinois, Oct. 16, 1854

Equal justice to the South, it is said, requires us to consent to the extending of slavery to new countries. That is to say, inasmuch as you do not object to my taking my hog to Nebraska, therefore I must not object to you taking your slave. Now, I admit this is perfectly logical, if there is no difference between hogs and Negroes. But while you thus require me to deny the humanity of the Negro, I wish to ask whether you of the South yourselves have ever been willing to do as much? It is kindly provided that of all those who come into the world, only a small percentage are natural tyrants. That percentage is no larger in the slave states than in the free. The great majority, South as well as North, have human sympathies, of which they can no more divest themselves than they can of their sensibility to physical pain. These sympathies in the bosoms of the Southern people, manifest in many ways, their sense of the wrong of slavery, and their consciousness that, after all, there is humanity in the Negro. If they deny this, let me address them a few plain questions. In 1820 you joined the North, almost unanimously, in declaring the African slave trade piracy, and in annexing to it the punishment of death. Why did you do this? If you did not feel that it was wrong, why did you join in providing that men should be hung for it? The practice was no more than bringing wild Negroes from Africa, to sell to such as would buy them. But you never thought of hanging men for catching and selling wild horses, wild buffaloes or wild bears.

Again, you have amongst you, a sneaking individual, of the class of native tyrants, known as the "Slave-Dealer." He watches your necessities, and crawls up to buy your slave, at a speculating price. If you cannot help it, you sell to him; but if you can help it, you drive him from your door. You despise him utterly. You do not recognize him as a friend, or even as an honest man. Your children must not play with his; they may rollick freely with the little Negroes, but not with the "slave-dealer's" children. If you are obliged to deal with him, you try to get through the job without so much as touching him. It is common with you to join hands with the men you meet; but with the slave dealer you avoid the ceremony—instinctively shrinking from the snaky contact. If he grows rich and retires from business, you still remember him, and still keep up the ban of non-intercourse upon him and his family. Now why is this? You do not so treat the man who deals in corn, cattle or tobacco.

Speech, Peoria, Illinois, Oct. 16, 1854

But one great argument in the support of the repeal of the Missouri Compromise is still to come. That argument is "the sacred right of self government." It seems our distinguished Senator [Douglas] has found great difficulty in getting his antagonists, even in the Senate to meet him fairly on this argument—some poet has said:

"Fools rush in where angels fear to tread."

At the hazard of being thought one of the fools of this quotation, I meet that argument—I rush in, I take that bull by the horns.

I trust I understand, and truly estimate the right of self-government. My faith in the proposition that each man should do precisely as he pleases with all which is exclusively his own, lies at the foundation of the sense of justice there is in me. I extend the principles to communities of men, as well as to individuals. I so extend it, because it is politically wise, as well as naturally just: politically wise, in saving us from broils about matters which do not concern us. Here, or at Washington, I would not trouble myself with the oyster laws of Virginia, or the cranberry laws of Indiana.

The doctrine of self-government is right—absolutely and eternally right—but it has no just application, as here attempted. Or perhaps I should rather say that whether it has such just application depends upon whether a Negro is *not* or *is* a man. If he is *not* a man, why, in that case, he who *is* a man may, as a matter of self-government, do just as he pleases with him. But if the Negro *is* a man, is it not to that extent, a total destruction of self-government, to say that he too shall not govern *himself*? When the white man governs himself that is self-government; but when he governs himself, and also governs *another* man, that is *more* than self-government—that is despotism. If the Negro is a *man*, why then my ancient faith teaches me that "all men are created equal"; and that there can be no moral right in connection with one man's making a slave of another.

Judge Douglas frequently, with bitter irony and sarcasm, paraphrases our argument by saying, "The white people of Nebraska are good enough to govern themselves, *but they are not good enough to govern a few miserable Negroes*!!"

Well, I doubt not that the people of Nebraska are, and will continue to be as good as the average of people elsewhere. I do not say the contrary. What I do say is, that no man is good enough to govern another man, *without that other's consent.* I say this is the leading principle—the sheet anchor of American republicanism.

Speech, Peoria, Illinois, Oct. 16, 1854

I am aware, you say, that taking slaves from the states to Nebraska does not make slaves of freemen; but the African slave trader can say just as much. He does not catch free Negroes and bring them here. He finds them already slaves in the hands of their black captors, and he honestly buys them at the rate of about a red cotton handkerchief a head. This is very cheap, and it is a great abridgment of the sacred right of self-government to hang men for engaging in this profitable trade.

Speech, Peoria, Illinois, Oct. 16, 1854

Let it not be said I am contending for the establishment of political and social equality between the whites and blacks. I have already said the contrary. I am not now combating the argument of NECESSITY, arising from the fact that the blacks are already amongst us; but I am combating what is set up as MORAL argument for allowing them to be taken where they have never yet been—arguing against the EXTENSION of a bad thing, which where it already exists, we must of necessity, manage as we best can.

In support of his application of the doctrine of self-government, Senator Douglas has sought to bring to his aid the opinions and examples of our revolutionary fathers. I am glad he has done this. I love the sentiments of those old-time men; and shall be most happy to abide by their opinions. He shows us that when it was in contemplation for the colonies to break off from Great Britain, and set up a new Government for themselves, several of the states instructed their delegates to go for the measure PROVIDED EACH STATE SHOULD BE ALLOWED TO REGULATE ITS DOMESTIC CONCERNS IN ITS OWN WAY. I do not quote; but this in substance. This was right. I see nothing objectionable in it. I also think it probable that it had some reference to the existence of slavery amongst them. I will not deny that it had. But had it, in any reference to the carrying of slavery into NEW COUNTRIES? That is the question; and we will let the fathers themselves answer it.

This same generation of men, and mostly the same individuals of the generation, who declared this principle—who declared independence—who fought the war of the revolution through—who afterwards made the Constitution under which we still live—these same men passed the ordinance of '87, declaring that slavery should never go to the northwest territory. I have no doubt Judge Douglas thinks they were very inconsistent in this. It is a question of discrimination between them and him. But there is not an inch of ground left for his claiming that their opinions—their example—their authority—are on his side in this controversy.

Letter to Horace Greeley, Aug. 22, 1862

I shall try to correct errors when shown to be errors, and I shall adopt new views so fast as they shall appear to be true views . . . and I intend no modification of my oft-expressed personal wish that all men everywhere could be free.

Fragment, Aug. 1, 1858?

As I would not be a *slave*, so I would not be a *master*. This expresses my idea of democracy. Whatever differs from this, to the extent of the difference, is no democracy.

Letter to Henry L. Pierce and Others, April 6, 1859

This is a world of compensation; and he who would be no slave must consent to have no slave. Those who deny freedom to others deserve it not for themselves, and, under a just God, cannot long retain it.

ESTATE SALE,

By order of the Executors of the late Dr. J. W. SCHMIDT.

By ALONZO J. WHITE.

On TUESDAY, the 17th day of January, 1854, at the North of the Custom House, at 11 o'clock, will be sold in Families, the following entire gang of

101 PRIME NEGROES.

CONDITIONS :—One third cash, balance in three equal annual instalments, with interest from day of sale, payable annually, secured by Bonds and Mortgage of Property sold, and approved personal security.—Purchasers to pay for requisite papers.

No.	Names.	Remarks.	Years of age.	No.	Names.	Remarks.	Years of age.
1	Kate,	Old Nurse,	75	52	Stepney,		24
2	Anthony,	Driver,	50	53	Rinah,		19
3	Rachael,	His Wife,	35	2—			
4	Clandee		8				
5	Ned		5	54	Betty,		50
6	Will		3	55	Harry,		30
7	Kitchey,	(12 months.)		56	Ellick,		55
7—				3—			
8	Joshua,		23	57	Little Billy,	(left thumb off.)	60
9	Rose,	His wife,	22	58	Venus,		75
10	Elsey,	Child	3	59	Gillam,		40
11	Cyrus,	Infant.		60	Sarah,	(his wife,	45
4—				61	Bella,		15
				62	Amaritta,		12
12	Nat		26	6—			
13	Charles,		7				
14	Elsey,		21	63	Scipio,		28
3—				1—			
15	Frank,		28	64	Jess,		50
16	Linda,	His wife,	25	65	Thomas,		14
17	Anthony,		6	66	Jesney,	a boy,	12
18	Boston,	Infant.		67	Betsey,		9
4—				4—			
19	Hector,		28	68	Jacob,		38
20	Hannah,	His wife,	26	69	Sue,		30
21	Hester		12	70	Fanny,		16
22	Harriet,		9	71	Patty,		12
23	Martha,		6	72	Harry,		11
24	Henry,		2	73	Caroline.		7
6—				74	Billy,	(deformed,)	9
				75	Isaac,		3
25	Jack,	Carpenter,	50	76	Lucy,	Infant,	
1—				9—			
26	Guinea Ben,	Cattle minder,	60	77	Hercules,		18
27	Luben,	Trusty Butler,	45	1—			
28	Jinney,	His wife,	28				
29	John,		14	78	Boston,	(Carpenter),	50
30	Ben,		12	79	Rosannah,		40
31	Celia,		8	80	Grace,		75
32	William,		6	81	John,		19
33	Margaret,		4	82	Miley,		12
34	James,		3	83	Stephen,		1½
35	Sol,	Infant.		84	Venus,		10
10—				7—			
36	Emanuel,		30	85	Joe,	(Carpenter, ruptured,)	50
37	Binah,		26	1—			
2—				86	Saby,		40
38	Cudjoe,		26	87	Mary,		30
39	Maria,		24	88	Hannah,		14
40	Mary,	Infant.		89	Boney,		12
3—				90	Morris,		4
				91	Sancho,		2
41	Isaac,		20	6—			
1—				92	Tom,		60
				1—			
42	Big Billy,		60				
43	Moses,	his children,	20	93	Toney,		18
44	Kate,	" "	18	94	Bram,		14
45	Abraham,	" "	12	2—			
46	Davey,	" "	10				
5—				95	John,	One straight finger,	28
				96	Lizzy,		26
47	Ben,		35	97	August,		8
48	Lydia,		30	98	Jacob,		2
49	Paul,		9	99	Mary,	Infant.	
50	Gilbert,		4				
51	Abby,	Infant.		100	Brutus,		60
5—				101	Nelly,	Cook,	80

Announcement of a slave auction, 1854.

$200 REWARD.

I will give the above reward for the apprehension of Ludwell, if taken in the state of Pennsylvania or any other Northern State and secured so that he is delivered to me or my agent; or $150 if taken in the State of Maryland or the District of Columbia. Ludwell ran away from Waverly, near the Warrenton Springs, on the 21st of October; he is 18 or 19 years old, dark complexion, about $5\frac{1}{2}$ feet high, and walks rather awkwardly and sluggishly. Had on when he left a dark colored sack coat, light pantaloons, a dark cloth cap and boots. He left in company with a slave of Mr. Parr's, of Culpeper County, who, I understand, is of low statue and black.

JOHN W. TYLER,
Warrenton, Fauquier Co., Va.
Oct. 28, 1854.

Poster offering a reward for the return of a runaway slave, 1854.

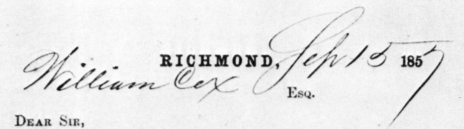

RICHMOND, Sep 15 185 7

William Cox Esq.

DEAR SIR,

The following is the state of our NEGRO MARKET to-day.

No. 1 Men,	Extra,	- - -	$1450 to 1550
" 1 "	Only,	- - -	1300 " 1400
" 2 "	Good,	- - -	1200 " 1250
" 2 "	Common,	- - -	1100 " 1150
" 1 Women,	Extra, 16 to 22 years of age, -		1200 " 1250
" 1 "	Only,	- - -	1100 " 1150
" 2 "	Good,	- -	1000 " 1050
" 2 "	Common,	- -	925 " 975
" 1 Boys,	4 feet	high, -	500 " 550
" 1 "	4 " 3 inches "	-	625 " 675
" 1 "	4 " 6 " "	-	750 " 850
" 1 "	4 " 9 " "	-	900 " 1000
" 1 "	5 " "	-	1050 " 1150
" 1 "	5 " 6 " "	-	1200 " 1250
" 1 Girls,	4 " "	-	500 " 550
" 1 "	4 " 3 " "	-	625 " 650
" 1 "	4 " 6 " "	-	750 " 800
" 1 "	4 " 9 " "	-	900 " 975
" 1 "	5 " "	-	1000 " 1075

Families & Scrubs sell in their usual proportion to Above quotations, We would be pleased to see you down soon with a likely lot

Very truly

D. M. Pulliam & Co

A slave dealer's market listing dated September, 1857.

Speech to 140th Indiana Regiment, March 17, 1865

I have always thought that all men should be free; but if any should be slaves, it should be first those who desire it for themselves, and secondly those who desire it for others. Whenever [I] hear anyone arguing for slavery, I feel a strong impulse to see it tried on him personally.

Fragment on Slavery, July 1, 1854?

. . . The most dumb and stupid slave that ever toiled for a master, does constantly *know* that he is wronged. So plain that no one, high or low, ever does mistake it, except in a plainly *selfish* way; for although volume upon volume is written to prove slavery a very good thing, we never hear of the man who wishes to take the good of it, *by being a slave himself.*

Most *governments* have been based, practically, on the denial of equal rights of men, as I have, in part, stated them; *ours* began, by *affirming* those rights. *They* said, some men are too *ignorant*, and *vicious*, to share in government. Possibly so, said we; and, by your system, you would always keep them ignorant, and vicious. We proposed to give *all* a chance; and we expected the weak to grow stronger, the ignorant, wiser; and all better, and happier together.

We made the experiment; and the fruit is before us.

Letter to Lieutenant Colonel John Glenn, Feb. 7, 1865

Complaint is made to me that you are forcing Negroes into the military service, and even torturing them—riding them on rails and the like—to extort their consent. I hope this may be a mistake. The like must not be done by you, or anyone under you. You must not force Negroes any more than white men. Answer me on this.

Emancipation Proclamation, Washington, D.C., Jan. 1, 1863

Whereas, on the twenty-second day of September, in the year of our Lord one thousand eight hundred and sixty-two, a proclamation was issued by the President of the United States, containing, among other things, the following, to wit:

"That on the first day of January, in the year of our Lord one thousand eight hundred and sixty-three, all persons held as slaves within any state, or designated part of a state, the people whereof shall then be in rebellion against the United States, shall be

then, thenceforward, and forever free; and the Executive Government of the United States, including the military and naval authority thereof, will recognize and maintain the freedom of such persons, and will do no act or acts to repress such persons, or any of them, in any efforts they may make for their actual freedom."

Letter to James C. Conkling, Aug. 26, 1863

You dislike the emancipation proclamation, and perhaps would have it retracted. You say it is unconstitutional. I think differently. I think the Constitution invests its commander-in-chief with the law of war in time of war. The most that can be said—if so much—is that slaves are property. Is there—has there ever been—any question that by the law of war, property, both of enemies and friends, may be taken when needed? And is it not needed whenever taking it helps us, or hurts the enemy?

Letter to Salmon P. Chase, Sept. 2, 1863

The original proclamation has no constitutional or legal justification, except as a military measure. The exemptions were made because the military necessity did not apply to the exempted localities. Nor does that necessity apply to them now any more than it did then. If I take the step, must I not do so without the arguments of military necessity, and so without any argument except the one that I think the measure politically expedient and morally right? Would I not thus give up all footing upon Constitution or law? Would I not thus be in the boundless field of absolutism? Could this pass unnoticed or unresisted?

Address on Colonization to a Deputation of Negroes, Aug. 14, 1862

. . . Why . . . should the people of your race be colonized? . . . You and we are different races. We have between us a broader difference than exists between almost any other two races. Whether it is right or wrong I need not discuss, but this physical difference is a great disadvantage to us both, as I think your race suffer very greatly, many of them by living among us, while ours suffer from your presence. In a word we suffer on each side. If this is admitted, it affords a reason at least why we should be separated. . . . I suppose one of the principal difficulties in the way of colonization is that the free colored man cannot see that his comfort would be advanced by it. You may believe you can live in Washington or elsewhere in the

United States the remainder of your life [as easily], perhaps more so than you can in any foreign country, and hence you may come to the conclusion that you have nothing to do with the idea of going to a foreign country. This is (I speak in no unkind sense) an extremely selfish view of the case.

But you ought to do something to help those who are not so fortunate as yourselves. . . . If we deal with those who are not free at the beginning, and whose intellects are clouded by slavery, we have very poor materials to start with. If intelligent colored men, such as are before me, would move in this matter, much might be accomplished. It is exceedingly important that we have men at the beginning capable of thinking as white men, and not those who have been systematically oppressed. . . .

For the sake of your race you should sacrifice something of your present comfort for the purpose of being as grand in that respect as the white people. . . . It is difficult to make a man miserable while he feels he is worthy of himself and claims kindred to the great God who made him.

All persons held as slaves shall be thenceforward and forever free . . .

Lincoln's words gave life to the struggle for human dignity.

IV

THE CAMPAIGN OF 1860

Immediately after the 1858 senatorial campaign, Lincoln began receiving letters from national figures along with invitations to speak throughout the nation. Lincoln, in reply to Republican leaders, counseled against their expressing private opinions unless the whole party could stand on them, because of the great variety of opinion within the new party. He warned against the excesses of the abolitionists and praised the liberal principles of Thomas Jefferson.

In his speeches he carried on the debates of 1858. It was in his famous speech at the Cooper Institute in New York that he spoke as a Presidential contender. The speech was enthusiastically received and was given much attention in the New York papers.

The politically adept Lincoln wisely chose not to make a premature, official announcement of his candidacy. Instead he decided to try to become the second choice of national convention delegates whose first choices were men such as Senator William H. Seward of New York, the acknowledged leader of the party. Lincoln was nominated on the third ballot at the convention in Chicago because, unlike Seward, who was marked as a radical, Lincoln could not be shown to be either conservative or radical. Also helpful were promises by Lincoln supporters of cabinet posts to key delegates—against Lincoln's expressed instructions.

Lincoln, in keeping with tradition, remained in Springfield and did not campaign for himself. He won the election due to efficient Republican organization, the stumping for Lincoln by the disappointed Seward and the North-South split in the Democratic Party (see Appendix). Lincoln won only a minority of the popular vote but he would have had a majority in the electoral college even if all opposition votes had gone to one man. During the months between his election and inauguration he continued to be publicly silent, believing that he had already made his views clear. But his inaugural address—which denounced secession as anarchy while disclaiming any intention of interfering with slavery in the Southern states—was conciliatory.

An August, 1860 political cartoon offered one publication's view
of Lincoln and the explosive slavery issue.

Address at Cooper Institute, New York, New York, Feb. 27, 1860

Wh! is the frame of Government under which we live?

The answer must be: "The Constitution of the United States." That Constitution consists of the original, framed in 1787 (and under which the present Government first went into operation), and 12 subsequently framed amendments, the first 10 of which were framed in 1789.

Who were our fathers that framed the Constitution? I suppose the "thirty-nine" who signed the original instrument may be fairly called our fathers who framed that part of the present Government. It is almost exactly true to say they framed it, and it is altogether true to say they fairly. represented the opinion and sentiment of the whole nation at that time. Their names, being familiar to nearly all, and accessible to quite all, need not now be repeated.

I take these "thirty-nine" for the present, as being "our fathers who framed the Government under which we live."

What is the question which, according to the text, those fathers understood "just as well, and even better than we do now?"

It is this: Does the proper division of local from Federal authority, or anything in the Constitution, forbid our Federal Government to control as to slavery in our Federal Territories?

Upon this, Senator Douglas holds the affirmative, and Republicans the negative. This affirmation and denial form an issue; and this issue—this question—is precisely what the text declares our fathers understood "better than we."

Let us now inquire whether the "thirty-nine," or any of them, ever acted upon this question; and if they did, how they acted upon it—how they expressed that better understanding? . . .

The sum of the whole is, that of our 39 fathers who framed the original Constitution, 21—a clear majority of the whole—certainly understood that no proper division of local from Federal authority, nor any part of the Constitution, forbade the Federal Government to control slavery in the Federal territories; while all the rest probably had the same understanding. Such, unquestionably, was the understanding of our fathers who framed the original Constitution; and the text affirms that they understood the question "better than we."

But, so far, I have been considering the understanding of the question manifested by the framers of the original Constitution. In and by the original instrument, a mode was provided for amending it; and, as I have already stated, the present frame of "the Government under which we live" consists of that original, and 12 amendatory articles framed and adopted since. Those who now insist that Federal control of slavery in Federal territories violates the Constitution, point us to the provisions which they suppose it thus violates; and, as I understand, they all fix upon provisions in these amendatory articles, and not in the original instrument. The Supreme Court, in the Dred Scott case, plant themselves upon the fifth amendment, which provides that no person shall be deprived of "life, liberty or property without due process of law"; while Senator Douglas and his peculiar adherents plant themselves upon the tenth amendment, providing that "the powers not delegated to the United States by the Constitution," "are reserved to the states respectively, or to the people."

Now, it so happens that these amendments were framed by the first Congress which sat under the Constitution—the identical Congress which passed the act already mentioned, enforcing the prohibition of slavery in the Northwestern Territory. . . .

Now, and here, let me guard a little against being misunderstood. I do not mean to say we are bound to follow implicitly in whatever our fathers did. To do so, would be to discard all the lights of current experience—to reject all progress—all improvement. What I do say is, that if we would supplant the opinions and policy of our fathers in any case, we should do so upon evidence so conclusive, and argument so clear, that even their great authority, fairly considered and weighed, cannot stand; and most surely not in a case whereof we ourselves declare they understood the question better than we. . . .

Let all who believe that "our fathers, who framed the Government under which we live, understood this question just as well, and even better, than we do now," speak as they spoke, and act as they acted upon it. This is all Republicans ask—all Republicans desire—in relation to slavery. As those fathers marked it, so let it be again marked, as an evil not to be extended, but to be tolerated and protected only because of and so far as its actual presence among us makes that toleration and protection a necessity. Let all the guaranties those fathers gave it, be, not grudgingly, but fully and fairly maintained. For this Republicans contend, and with this, so far as I know or believe, they will be content.

And now, if they would listen—as I suppose they will not—I would address a few words to the Southern people. . . .

. . . You say you are conservative—eminently conservative—while we are revolutionary, destructive, or something of the sort. What is conservatism? Is it not adherence to the old and tried, against the new and untried? We stick to, contend for, the identical old policy on the point in controversy which was adopted by "our fathers who framed the Government under which we live"; while you with one accord reject, and scout, and spit upon that old policy, and insist upon substituting something new. . . .

Much is said by Southern people about the affection of slaves for their masters and mistresses; and a part of it, at least, is true. . . .

In the language of Mr. Jefferson, uttered many years ago, "It is still in our power to direct the process of emancipation, and deportation, peaceably, and in such slow degrees, as that the evil will wear off insensibly; and their places be, *pari passu*, filled up by free white laborers. If, on the contrary, it is left to force itself on, human nature must shudder at the prospect held up."

Mr. Jefferson did not mean to say, nor do I, that the power of emancipation is in the Federal Government. He spoke of Virginia; and, as to the power of emancipation, I speak of the slaveholding states only. The Federal Government, however, as we insist, has the power of restraining the extension of the institution—the power to insure that a slave insurrection shall never occur on any American soil which is now free from slavery. . . .

There is a judgment and a feeling against slavery in this nation, which cast at least a million and a half of votes. You cannot destroy that judgment and feeling—that sentiment—by breaking up the political organization which rallies around it. You can scarcely

Many groups rallied to support Lincoln during the 1860 campaign.

scatter and disperse an army which has been formed into order in the face of your heaviest fire; but if you could, how much would you gain by forcing the sentiment which created it out of the peaceful channel of the ballot-box, into some other channel? What would that other channel probably be? Would the number of John Browns be lessened or enlarged by the operation?

But you will break up the Union rather than submit to a denial of your constitutional rights.

That has a somewhat reckless sound; but it would be palliated, if not fully justified, were we proposing, by the mere force of numbers, to deprive you of some right, plainly written down in the Constitution. But we are proposing no such thing. . . .

Your purpose . . . is that you will destroy the Government, unless you be allowed to construe and enforce the Constitution as you please, on all points in dispute between you and us. You will rule or ruin in all events.

This, plainly stated, is your language. Perhaps you will say the Supreme Court has decided the disputed constitutional question in your favor.* Not quite so. . . . The Court have decided the question for you in a sort of way. The Court have substantially said, it is your constitutional right to take slaves into the Federal territories, and to hold them there as property. When I say the decision was made in a sort of way, I mean it was made in a divided Court, by a bare majority of the judges, and they not quite agreeing with one another in the reasons for making it, that it is so made as that its avowed supporters disagree with one another about its meaning, and that it was mainly based upon a mistaken statement of fact—the statement in the opinion that "the right of property in a slave is distinctly and expressly affirmed in the Constitution. . . ."

A few words now to Republicans. It is exceedingly desirable that all parts of this great Confederacy shall be at peace, and in harmony, one with another. Let us Republicans do our part to have it so. Even though much provoked, let us do nothing through passion and ill temper. Even though the Southern people will not so much as listen to us, let us calmly consider their demands, and yield to them if, in our deliberate view of our duty, we possibly can. . . .

If slavery is right, all words, acts, laws and constitutions against it are themselves wrong, and should be silenced, and swept away. If it is right, we cannot justly object to its nationality—its universality; if it

is wrong, they cannot justly insist upon its extension—its enlargement. All they ask, we could readily grant, if we thought slavery right; all we ask, they could as readily grant, if they thought it wrong. Their thinking it right, and our thinking it wrong, is the precise fact upon which depends the whole controversy. Thinking it right, as they do, they are not to blame for desiring its full recognition, as being right; but, thinking it wrong, as we do, can we yield to them? Can we cast our votes with their view, and against our own? In view of our moral, social and political responsibilities, can we do this?

Wrong as we think slavery is, we can yet afford to let it alone where it is, because that much is due to the necessity arising from its actual presence in the nation; but can we, while our votes will prevent it, allow it to spread into the national territories, and to overrun us here in these free states? If our sense of duty forbids this, then let us stand by our duty, fearlessly and effectively. Let us be diverted by none of those sophistical contrivances wherewith we are so industriously plied and belabored—contrivances such as groping for some middle ground between the right and the wrong, vain as the search for a man who should be neither a living man nor a dead man—such as a policy of "don't care" on a question about which all true men do care—such as Union appeals beseeching true Union men to yield to disunionists, reversing the divine rule, and calling, not the sinners, but the righteous to repentance—such as invocations to Washington, imploring men to unsay what Washington said, and undo what Washington did.

Neither let us be slandered from our duty by false accusations against us, nor frightened from it by menaces of destruction to the Government nor of dungeons to ourselves. LET US HAVE FAITH THAT RIGHT MAKES MIGHT, AND IN THAT FAITH, LET US, TO THE END, DARE TO DO OUR DUTY AS WE UNDERSTAND IT.

Imaginary Dialogue Written by Lincoln, Sept. 29, 1860

Meeting & Dialogue of Douglas & Breckinridge*

DOUG—Well, you have succeeded in breaking up the Democratic party.

BRECK—Certainly, for the time being, the party is under a cloud, to say the least; but why you should say *I* did it, I do not comprehend.

DOUG—Perhaps I should charge it to your *supporters*, rather than to *you*.

BRECK—The blame, as I conceive, is neither upon my friends or me.

---

*Lincoln is referring to the Supreme Court's Dred Scott decision of 1857 which claimed that Negroes were not U.S. citizens and thus came under the Constitution only as property.

---

*John C. Breckinridge (Ky.) was Presidential candidate of the Independent Democratic Party (see Appendix).

Let us have faith that right makes might . . .

Lincoln liked his post-Presidential nomination portrait by Hesler.
". . . If it pleases the people I am satisfied," he said.

DOUG—They insisted on having a platform, upon which *I* could not stand.

BRECK—Aye, and *you* insisted on having a platform upon which *they* could not stand.

DOUG—But *mine* was the true *Democratic* platform.

BRECK—That presents the exact point in dispute; my friends insist that *theirs* is the true Democratic platform.

DOUG—Let us argue it, then.

BRECK—I conceive that argument is exhausted; *you* certainly could advance nothing new, and *I* know not that I could. There ,is, however, a collateral point, upon which I would like the exchange of a few words.

DOUG—What is it?

BRECK—It is this: We insisted on Congressional protection of slave property in the national territories; and you broke with us professedly because of this.

DOUG—Exactly so; I insisted upon non-intervention.

BRECK—And yet you are forming coalitions, wherever you can, with Bell, who is for this very Congressional protection of slavery—for the very thing which you pretend, drove you from us—for Bell, with all his Know-Nothingism, and anti-democracy of every sort.

DOUG—Bell is a good Union-man; and you, and your friends, are a set of disunionists.

BRECK—Bah! You have known us long, and intimately; why did you never denounce us as disunionists, till since our refusal to support *you* for the Presidency? Why have you never warned the North against our disunion schemes, till since the Charleston and Baltimore sessions of the National Convention? Will you answer, Senator Douglas?

DOUG—The condition of my throat will not permit me to carry this conversation any further.

First Inaugural Address, Washington, D.C., March 4, 1861

Fellow-citizens of the United States: In compliance with a custom as old as the Government itself, I appear before you to address you briefly, and to take, in your presence, the oath prescribed by the Constitution of the United States to be taken by the President "before he enters on the execution of his office". . . .

I do not consider it necessary at present for me to discuss those matters of administration about which there is no special anxiety or excitement.

Apprehension seems to exist among the people of the Southern states that by the accession of a Republican Administration their property and their peace and personal security are to be endangered. There has never been any reasonable cause for such apprehen-sion. Indeed, the most ample evidence to the contrary has all the while existed and been open to their inspection. It is found in nearly all the published speeches of him who now addresses you. I do but quote from one of those speeches when I declare that "I have no purpose, directly or indirectly, to interfere with the institution of slavery in the states where it exists. I believe I have no lawful right to do so, and I have no inclination to do so." Those who nominated and elected me did so with full knowledge that I had made this, and many similar declarations, and had never recanted them. And, more than this, they placed in the platform for my acceptance, and as a law to themselves, and to me, the clear and emphatic resolu-tion which I now read:

"*Resolved*, That the maintenance inviolate of the rights of the states, and especially the right of each state to order and control its own domestic institu-tions according to its own judgment exclusively, is essential to that balance of power on which the perfec-tion and endurance of our political fabric depend; and we denounce the lawless invasion by armed force of the soil of any state or territory, no matter under what pretext, as among the gravest of crimes."

I now reiterate these sentiments; and, in doing so, I only press upon the public attention the most con-clusive evidence of which the case is susceptible, that the property, peace and security of no section are to be in anywise endangered by the now incoming Administration. I add, too, that all the protection which, consistently with the Constitution and the laws, can be given, will be cheerfully given to all the states when lawfully demanded, for whatever cause—as cheerfully to one section, as to another. . . .

I take the official oath today with no mental reservations and with no purpose to construe the Constitution or laws by any hypercritical rules. And while I do not choose now to specify particular acts of Congress as proper to be enforced, I do suggest that it will be much safer for all, both in official and private stations, to conform to and abide by all those acts which stand unrepealed, than to violate any of them trusting to find impunity in having them held to be unconstitutional.

It is 72 years since the first inauguration of a President under our national Constitution. During that period 15 different and greatly distinguished citi-zens have, in succession, administered the executive branch of the Government. They have conducted it through many perils, and generally with great success. Yet with all this scope of precedent, I now enter upon the same task for the brief constitutional term of four years under great and peculiar difficulty. A disruption of the Federal Union, heretofore only menaced, is now formidably attempted.

I hold that, in contemplation of universal law and of the Constitution, the Union of these States is perpetual. Perpetuity is implied, if not expressed, in the fundamental law of all national governments. It is safe to assert that no government proper ever had a provision in its organic law for its own termination. Continue to execute all the express provisions of our national Constitution, and the Union will endure forever—it being impossible to destroy it except by some action not provided for in the instrument itself. . . .

Descending from these general principles, we find the proposition that, in legal contemplation, the Union is perpetual, confirmed by the history of the Union itself. The Union is much older than the Constitution. It was formed, in fact, by the Articles of Association in 1774. It was matured and continued by the Declaration of Independence in 1776. It was further matured, and the faith of all the then 13 states expressly plighted and engaged that it should be perpetual, by the Articles of Confederation in 1778. And, finally, in 1787, one of the declared objects for ordaining and establishing the Constitution was "to form a more perfect Union."

But if the destruction of the Union by one, or by a part only, of the states be lawfully possible, the Union is less perfect than before the Constitution, having lost the vital element of perpetuity.

It follows from these views that no state, upon its own mere motion, can lawfully get out of the Union, —that resolves and ordinances to that effect are legally void; and that acts of violence, within any state or states, against the authority of the United States, are insurrectionary or revolutionary, according to circumstances.

I therefore consider that, in view of the Constitution and the laws, the Union is unbroken; and, to the extent of my ability, I shall take care, as the Constitution itself expressly enjoins upon me, that the laws of the Union be faithfully executed in all of the states. . . .

In doing this there needs to be no bloodshed or violence; and there shall be none, unless it be forced upon the national authority. . . .

Plainly, the central idea of secession is the essence of anarchy. A majority held in restraint by constitutional checks and limitations, and always changing easily with deliberate changes of popular opinions and sentiments, is the only true sovereign of a free people. Whoever rejects it does, of necessity, fly to anarchy or to despotism. Unanimity is impossible; the rule of a minority, as a permanent arrangement, is wholly inadmissible; so that, rejecting the majority principle, anarchy or despotism in some form is all that is left. . . .

This country, with its institutions, belongs to the people who inhabit it. Whenever they shall grow weary of the existing Government, they can exercise their *constitutional* right of amending it, or their *revolutionary* right to dismember or overthrow it. . . .

The Chief Magistrate derives all his authority from the people, and they have conferred none upon him to fix terms for the separation of the states. The people themselves can do this also if they choose; but the Executive, as such, has nothing to do with it. His duty is to administer the present Government, as it came to his hands, and to transmit it, unimpaired by him, to his successor. . . .

While the people retain their virtue, and vigilance, no Administration, by any extreme of wickedness or folly, can very seriously injure the Government, in the short space of four years. . . .

In *your* hands, my dissatisfied fellow countrymen, and not in *mine*, is the momentous issue of civil war. The Government will not assail *you*. You can have no conflict without being yourselves the aggressors. *You* have no oath registered in Heaven to destroy the Government, while *I* shall have the most solemn one to "preserve, protect and defend it."

I am loth to close. We are not enemies, but friends. We must not be enemies. Though passion may have strained, it must not break our bonds of affection. The mystic chords of memory, stretching from every battlefield and patriot grave to every living heart and hearthstone all over this broad land, will yet swell the chorus of the Union, when again touched, as surely they will be, by the better angels of our nature.

Bust of Lincoln, Capitol Rotunda, Washington, D.C.

V

LINCOLN,

THE UNION AND THE PRESIDENCY

Lincoln became President at the most crucial moment in American history. The day he was inaugurated eight states had already announced that they had seceded and war was imminent. Yet Lincoln, elected by a minority of the popular vote, came to office after a decade during which the United States had endured its three consecutively weakest Presidents—Millard Fillmore, Franklin Pierce, James Buchanan—and the departments of the executive branch of the Federal Government were unused to serving few purposes other than patronage and self-aggrandizement. As he faced these massive problems Lincoln had several important handicaps of his own: He was inexperienced as an administrator and untrained in executive functions. He had never held an elective office higher than state legislator—except for an undistinguished two-year term as Congressman which had ended twelve years before. He had chosen his cabinet to represent all major Republican factions so that several cabinet members were antagonistic toward each other, a few were outright enemies and some considered Lincoln distinctly inferior to themselves.

In his first weeks as President, Lincoln seemed to fulfill the worst fears of the nation. But, after several weeks of vacillation and muddling, he finally decided that Fort Sumter should not be surrendered and, with that decision, Lincoln began his development toward becoming a great President. He never became much of an administrator but he was an expert politician, a clear-headed thinker and a wise and courageous leader who knew when to be immovably firm and when to loosen the reins. By the end of his Presidency he had repaired the diminished power and dissipated prestige of the office and had given it a new dimension with his concept of its war power.

In some matters, such as the determination of suffrage, Lincoln believed in Federal non-intervention, but war was different. Lincoln turned to the "Commander-in-Chief" clause of the Constitution concluding that "the war power" was his. The first duty of the President is to preserve the Union and the Union was in danger as never before. In the latter part of his term, because of problems of emancipation and reconstruction, he came to the position that as President he had extraordinary legal resources lacked by Congress, a body which he considered little more than a necessary nuisance.

As he extended his powers, some accused him of being a dictator but, in general, he acted with restraint, considering the situation. His suspension of habeas corpus, for example, was used more as a preventative precaution than as a punitive weapon.

PRESIDENT'S HOUSE, WASHINGTON.

The White House as it appeared during Lincoln's residence.

From *Recollections of Abraham Lincoln, 1847–1865,*
by Ward H. Lamon

You know better than any man living that from my boyhood up my ambition was to be President. I am President of one part of this divided country at least; but look at me! I wish I had never been born! It is a white elephant on my hands, and hard to manage. With a fire in my front and rear; having to contend with the jealousies of the military commanders, and not receiving that cordial cooperation and support from Congress which could reasonably be expected; with an active and formidable enemy in the field threatening the very life-blood of the Government—my position is anything but a bed of roses.

From *Recollections of Abraham Lincoln, 1847–1865,*
by Ward H. Lamon

In God's name! If any one can do better in my place than I have done, or am endeavoring to do, let him try his hand at it, and no one will be better contented than myself.

Remarks at Lawrenceburg, Indiana, Feb. 12, 1861

I have been selected to fill an important office for a brief period, and am now, in your eyes, invested with an influence which will soon pass away; but should my Administration prove to be a very wicked one, or what is more probable, a very foolish one, if you, the people, are but true to yourselves and to the Constitution, there is but little harm I can do, *thank God!*

Reply to Massachusetts Delegation, March 5, 1861

As the President in the administration of the Government, I hope to be man enough not to know one citizen of the United States from another, nor one section from another.

To Leonard Swett. From *Herndon's Lincoln: The True Story of a Great Life,* by William H. Herndon and Jesse Weik

I may not have made as great a President as some other man, but I believe I have kept these discordant elements together as well as anyone could.

To a caller at the White House.
From *Lincoln's Yarns and Stories*, by Alexander McClure

If you once forfeit the confidence of your fellow citizens, you can never regain their respect and esteem. It is true that you may fool all the people some of the time; you can even fool some of the people all the time; but you can't fool all of the people all the time.

Letter to Matthew Birchard and Others, June 29, 1863

You ask, in substance, whether I really claim that I may override all the guaranteed rights of individuals, on the plea of conserving the public safety—when I may choose to say the public safety requires it. This question, divested of the phraseology calculated to represent me as struggling for an arbitrary personal prerogative, is either simply a question *who* shall decide, or an affirmation that *nobody* shall decide, what the public safety does require in cases of rebellion or invasion.

The Constitution contemplates the question as likely to occur for decision, but it does not expressly declare who is to decide it. By necessary implication, when rebellion or invasion comes, the decision is to be made from time to time; and I think the man whom, for the time, the people have, under the Constitution, made the commander-in-chief of their army and navy, is the man who holds the power and bears the responsibility of making it. If he uses the power justly, the same people will probably justify him; if he abuses it, he is in their hands to be dealt with by all the modes they have reserved to themselves in the Constitution.

Letter to Erastus Corning and Others, June 12, 1863

They [secessionists and sympathizers] knew that in times such as they were inaugurating, by the Constitution itself the habeas corpus might be suspended; but they also knew they had friends who would make a question as to who was to suspend it; meanwhile their spies and others might remain at large to help on their cause. Or if, as has happened, the Executive should suspend the writ without ruinous waste of time, instances of arresting innocent persons might occur, as are always likely to occur in such cases; and then a clamor could be raised in regard to this, which might be at least of some service to the insurgent cause. It needed no very keen perception to discover this part of the enemy's program, so soon as by open hostilities their machinery was fairly put in motion. Yet, thoroughly imbued with a reverence for the guaranteed rights of individuals, I was slow to adopt the strong measures which by degrees I have been forced to regard as being within the exceptions of the Constitution, and as indispensable to the public safety. Nothing is better known to history than that courts of justice are utterly incompetent [in] such cases. Civil courts are organized chiefly for trials of individuals, or, at most, a few individuals acting in concert—and this in quiet times, and on charges of crimes well defined in the law. Even in times of peace bands of horse-thieves and robbers frequently grow too numerous and powerful for the ordinary courts of justice. But what comparison, in numbers, have such bands ever borne to the insurgent sympathizers even in many of the loyal states? Again, a jury too frequently has at least one member more ready to hang the panel than to hang the traitor. And yet again, he who dissuades one man from volunteering, or induces one soldier to desert, weakens the Union cause as much as he who kills a Union soldier in battle. Yet this dissuasion or inducement may be so conducted as to be no defined crime of which any civil court would take cognizance.

Proclamation Suspending Writ of Habeas Corpus, Sept. 15, 1863

I . . . proclaim and make known to all whom it may concern that the privilege of the writ of habeas corpus is suspended throughout the United States in the several cases before mentioned [persons held under the command or in custody of military, naval or civil officers of the United States, "either as prisoners of war, spies, or aiders or abettors of the enemy, or officers or soldiers or seamen enrolled or drafted or mustered or enlisted in or belonging to the land of naval forces of the United States or as deserters there from, or otherwise amenable to military law or the rules or regulations prescribed for the military or naval services . . . or for resisting a draft or for any other offense against the military or naval service"] and that this suspension will continue throughout the duration of the said rebellion or until this proclamation shall, by a subsequent one to be issued by the President of the United States, be modified or revoked.

From *Recollections of Abraham Lincoln, 1847–1865*, by Ward H. Lamon

. . . These rebels are violating the Constitution to destroy the Union; I will violate the Constitution, if necessary, to save the Union: and I suspect . . . that our Constitution is going to have a rough time of it before we get done with this row.

Mt. McKinley National Park. The United States began
negotiating with Russia for purchase of Alaska before the Civil War.
Two years after Lincoln's assassination, his secretary of state,
William H. Seward, completed arrangements for the
purchase during his service as a cabinet member
under Lincoln's successor, Andrew Johnson.

Letter to Erastus Corning and Others, June 12, 1863

If I be wrong on this question of constitutional power, my error lies in believing that certain proceedings are constitutional when, in cases of rebellion or invasion, the public safety requires them, which would not be constitutional when, in absence of rebellion or invasion, the public safety does not require them: in other words, that the Constitution is not in its application in all respects the same in cases of rebellion or invasion involving the public safety, as it is in times of profound peace and public security. The Constitution itself makes the distinction, and I can no more be persuaded that the Government can constitutionally take no strong measures in time of rebellion, because it can be shown that the same could not be lawfully taken in time of peace, than I can be persuaded that a particular drug is not good medicine for a sick man because it can be shown to not be good food for a well one. Nor am I able to appreciate the danger apprehended by the meeting, that the American people will, by means of military arrests during the rebellion, lose the right of public discussion, the liberty of speech and the press, the law of evidence, trial by jury, and habeas corpus throughout the indefinite peaceful future which I trust lies before them, any more than I am able to believe that a man could contract so strong an appetite for emetics during temporary illness as to persist in feeding upon them during the remainder of his healthful life.

Response to a Serenade*, Nov. 10, 1864

It has long been a grave question whether any government, not too strong for the liberties of its people, can be strong enough to maintain its own existence in great emergencies.

Fragment on Government, July 1, 1854?

Why...should we have government? Why not each individual take to himself the whole fruit of his labor, without having any of it taxed away, in services, corn or money? Why not take just so much land as he can cultivate with his own hands, without buying it of anyone?

---

*A political serenade took place when a candidate's supporters gathered outside a place where he was staying and sang political songs favoring him and cheered him, usually until he addressed the throng.

The legitimate object of government is "to do for the people what needs to be done, but which they cannot, by individual effort, do at all, or do so well, for themselves." There are many such things—some of them exist independently of the injustice in the world. Making and maintaining roads, bridges and the like; providing for the helpless young and afflicted; common schools; and disposing of deceased men's property, are instances.

But a far larger class of objects springs from the injustice of men. If one people will make war upon another, it is a necessity with that other to unite and cooperate for defense. Hence the military department. If some men will kill, or beat, or constrain others, or despoil them of property, by force, fraud or noncompliance with contracts, it is a common object with peaceful and just men to prevent it. Hence the criminal and civil departments.

Fragment on Government, July 1, 1854?

. . . If all men were just, there still would be *some*, though not *so much*, need of government.

Speech, Springfield, Illinois, June 16, 1858

Mr. President and Gentlemen of the Convention:

If we could first know where we are, and whither we are tending, we could then better judge what to do, and how to do it.

We are now far into the fifth year, since a policy was initiated, with the avowed object, and confident promise, of putting an end to slavery agitation.

Under the operation of that policy, that agitation has not only not ceased, but has constantly augmented.

In my opinion, it will not cease until a crisis shall have been reached, and passed.

"A house divided against itself cannot stand."

I believe this Government cannot endure, permanently half slave and half free.

I do not expect the Union to be dissolved—I do not expect the house to fall—but I do expect it will cease to be divided.

It will become all one thing, or all the other.

Either the opponents of slavery will arrest the further spread of it, and place it where the public mind shall rest in the belief that it is in course of ultimate extinction; or its advocates will push it forward, till it shall become alike lawful in all the states, old as well as new—North as well as South. . . .

Our cause . . . must be intrusted to, and conducted by its own undoubted friends—those whose hands are free, whose hearts are in the work—who do care for the result.

Two years ago the Republicans of the nation mustered over thirteen hundred thousand strong.

We did this under the single impulse of resistance to a common danger, with every external circumstance against us.

Of strange, discordant, and even, hostile elements, we gathered from the four winds, and formed and fought the battle through, under the constant hot fire of a disciplined, proud and pampered enemy.

Did we brave all then, to falter now?—now—when that same enemy is wavering, dissevered and belligerent?

The result is not doubtful. We shall not fail—if we stand firm, we shall not fail.

Wise councils may accelerate or mistakes delay it, but sooner or later the victory is sure to come.

Letter to Horace Greeley, Aug. 22, 1862

My paramount object in this struggle is to save the Union, and is not either to save or to destroy slavery. If I could save the Union without freeing any slave, I would do it; and if I could save it by freeing all the slaves, I would do it; and if I could save it by freeing some and leaving others alone, I would also do that.

Reply to Mayor Fernando Wood, New York, New York, Feb. 20, 1861

There is nothing that can ever bring me willingly to consent to the destruction of this Union . . . unless it were to be that thing for which the Union itself was made. I understand a ship to be made for the carrying and preservation of the cargo; and so long as the ship can be saved with the cargo, it should never be abandoned. This Union should likewise never be abandoned unless it fails and the possibility of its preservation shall cease to exist without throwing the passengers and cargo overboard. So long, then, as it is possible that the prosperity and the liberties of the people can be preserved in the Union, it shall be my purpose at all times to preserve it.

Letter to Albert G. Hodges, April 4, 1864

. . . My oath to preserve the Constitution to the best of my ability imposed upon me the duty of preserving, by every indispensable means, that Government—that nation—of which that Constitution was the organic law. Was it possible to lose the nation, and yet preserve the Constitution? . . . I could not feel that, to the best of my ability, I had even tried to preserve the Constitution, if, to save slavery, or any minor matter, I should permit the wreck of Government, country and Constitution, all together.

Message to Congress, July 4, 1861

It might seem at first thought to be of little difference whether the present movement at the South be called "secession" or "rebellion." The movers, however, well understand the difference. At the beginning they knew they could never raise their treason to any respectable magnitude by any name which implies *violation* of law. . . . Accordingly, they commenced by an insidious debauching of the public mind. They invented an ingenious sophism, which, if conceded, was followed by perfectly logical steps through all the incidents to the complete destruction of the Union. The sophism itself is that any state of the Union may, *consistently* with the national Constitution, and therefore *lawfully* and *peacefully*, withdraw from the Union, without the consent of the Union, or of any other state. The little disguise that the supposed right is to be exercised only for just cause, themselves to be the sole judge of its justice, is too thin to merit any notice.

Letter to James C. Conkling, Aug. 26, 1863

. . . Among free men there can be no successful appeal from the ballot to the bullet, and . . . they who take such appeal are sure to lose their case and pay the cost.

Speech, Galena, Illinois, July 23, 1856

We, the majority, would not strive to dissolve the Union; and if any attempt is made it must be by you, who so loudly stigmatize us as disunionists. But the Union, in any event, won't be dissolved. We don't want to dissolve it, and if you attempt it, we won't let you. With the purse and sword, the army and navy and treasury in our hands and at our command, you couldn't do it. This Government would be very weak, indeed, if a majority, with a disciplined army and navy, and a well-filled treasury, could not preserve itself, when attacked by an unarmed, undisciplined, unorganized minority.

All this talk about the dissolution of the Union is humbug—nothing but folly. We won't dissolve the Union, and you shan't.

Letter to Reverdy Johnson, July 26, 1862

I am a patient man—always willing to forgive on the Christian terms of repentance, and also to give ample *time* for repentance. Still, I must save this Government, if possible. . . . It may as well be understood, once for all, that I shall not surrender this game, leaving any available cards unplayed.

A house divided against

itself cannot stand . . .

Lincoln statue by sculptress Vinnie Ream, Washington, D.C.

Bates   Welles. Blair. Seward. Chase.   Lincoln.   Scott.   Smith. Cameron.

An old lithograph shows Lincoln's first Army commander,
General Winfield Scott, addressing the President and his Cabinet.

Annual Message to Congress, Washington, D.C., Dec. 1, 1862

If there ever could be a proper time for mere catch arguments, that time surely is not now. In times like the present, men should utter nothing for which they would not willingly be responsible through time and in eternity.

Speech, Frederick, Maryland, Oct. 4, 1862

In my present position it is hardly proper for me to make speeches. Every word is so closely noted that it will not do to make trivial ones, and I cannot be expected to be prepared to make a matured one just now. If I were as I have been most of my life, I might perhaps, talk amusing to you for half an hour, and it wouldn't hurt anybody. . . .

Speech, Pittsburgh, Pennsylvania, Feb. 15, 1861

My advice . . . is to keep cool. If the great American people will only keep their temper on both sides of the line, the troubles will come to an end, and the question which now distracts the country will be settled just as surely as all other difficulties of like character which have originated in this Government have been adjusted. Let the people on both sides keep their self-possession, and just as other clouds have cleared away in due time, and so will this, and this great nation shall continue to prosper as heretofore.

Letter to Isaac M. Schermerhorn, Sept. 12, 1864

In taking the various steps which have led to my present position in relation to the war, the public interest and my private interest have been perfectly parallel, because in no other way could I serve myself so well as by truly serving the Union. The whole field has been open to me where to choose. No place-hunting necessity has been upon me urging me to seek a position of antagonism to some other man, irrespective of whether such position might be favorable or unfavorable to the Union.

Of course I may err in judgment, but my present position, in reference to the rebellion is the result of my best judgment, and, according to that best judgment, it is the only position upon which any executive can or could save the Union.

To Horace Maynard. From *Herndon's Lincoln: The True Story of a Great Life*, by William H. Herndon and Jesse Weik

I shall go just so fast and only so fast as I think I'm right and the people are ready for the step.

Conversation at the White House. From *The Inner Life of Abraham Lincoln: Six Months at the White House*, by Francis B. Carpenter

If I were to try to read, much less answer, all the attacks made on me this shop might as well be closed for any other business. I do the very best I know how—the very best I can; and I mean to keep doing so until the end. If the end brings me out all right, what is said against me won't amount to anything. If the end brings me out wrong 10 angels swearing I was right would make no difference.

From *Recollections of Abraham Lincoln, 1847–1865*, by Ward H. Lamon

I will show them at the other end of the Avenue [Congress] whether I am President or not!

From *Recollections of Abraham Lincoln, 1847–1865*, by Ward H. Lamon

I cannot run this thing [the Presidency] upon the theory that every officeholder must think I am the greatest man in the nation, and I will not.

Letter to Carl Schurz, Nov. 10, 1862

The Administration came into power, very largely in a minority of the popular vote. Notwithstanding this, it distributed to its party friends as nearly all the civil patronage as any Administration ever did.

Frank Leslie's Illustrated Weekly, Nov. 22, 1862

(*The President takes the result of the New York elections philosophically, and will, doubtless, profit by the lesson. When Colonel Forney inquired of him how he felt about New York, he replied:*) Somewhat like the boy in Kentucky, who stubbed his toe while running to see his sweetheart. The boy said he was too big to cry, and far too badly hurt to laugh.

Reply to a Serenade in Honor of the Emancipation Proclamation, Sept. 24, 1862

Yet they [the difficulties of the Presidency] are scarcely so great as the difficulties of those who, upon the battlefield, are endeavoring to purchase with their blood and their lives the future happiness and prosperity of this country.

Memorandum Concerning His Probable Failure of Re-election, Aug. 23, 1864

This morning, as for some days past, it seems exceedingly probable that this Administration will not be re-elected. Then it will be my duty to so cooperate with the President-elect as to save the Union between the election and the inauguration; as he will have secured his election on such ground that he cannot possibly save it afterward.

From *Recollections of Abraham Lincoln, 1847–1865*, by Ward H. Lamon

I have enough to look after without giving much of my time to the consideration of the subject of who shall be my successor in office. The position is not an easy one; and the occupant, whoever he may be, for the next four years, will have little leisure to pluck a thorn or plant a rose in his own pathway.

Address Before the Young Men's Lyceum, Springfield, Illinois, Jan. 27, 1838

Towering genius disdains a beaten path. It seeks regions hitherto unexplored.

Last Public Address, Washington, D.C., April 11, 1865

Important principles may, and must, be inflexible.

Annual Message to Congress, Washington, D.C., Dec. 1, 1862

Fellow-citizens, we cannot escape history. We of this Congress and this Administration will be remembered in spite of ourselves. No personal significance or insignificance can spare one or another of us. The fiery trial through which we pass will light us down, in honor or dishonor, to the latest generation. We say we are for the Union. The world will not forget that we say this. We know how to save the Union. The world knows we do know how to save it. We—even we here—hold the power and bear the responsibility. In giving freedom to the slave, we assure freedom to the free—honorable alike in what we give and what we preserve. We shall nobly save or meanly lose the last, best hope of earth. Other means may succeed; this could not fail. The way is plain, peaceful, generous, just—a way which, if followed, the world will forever applaud, and God must forever bless.

Letter to Albert G. Hodges, April 4, 1864

I claim not to have controlled events, but confess plainly that events have controlled me.

VI

LINCOLN AND THE CIVIL WAR

Although Lincoln's first inaugural speech was peaceful in tone, he had decided several months before against any compromise of principle. Compromise, he knew, was no guarantee of peace. "The tug has to come, and better now than any time hereafter," he said.

Once he had determined not to surrender Fort Sumter, he did not hesitate to prosecute the war, for he believed the war was a test to see if the American experiment of people governing themselves could successfully maintain itself by suppressing rebellion. He was convinced that the fate of world democracy hung on the fate of the Union. Such is the essence of his immortal address at Gettysburg.

At the beginning of the war, the South was much better prepared than the North and had a greater unity of purpose—independence. The North, however, had superiority in transportation, industry and population. Lincoln had to endure the inabilities of political generals such as Ben Butler because they controlled sizable segments of public opinion, but this was not as much of a hindrance as was the lack of a viable central government to the Confederacy. Once the Federal Government in Washington was organized—particularly the War Department under the irascible but efficient Stanton—the Union superiority began to be felt.

What was needed finally was a general who could command the Union armies to decisive victories. Lincoln patiently sifted through a series of generals including the hesitant George B. McClellan, Irvin McDowell, Joseph Hooker and George G. Meade, relieving each in turn. During this period Lincoln visited the Army of the Potomac repeatedly to confer with its commanders, but most of Lincoln's involvement in military matters proved unsuccessful, usually due to political pressures or unsatisfactory personnel. This involvement ceased when Lincoln found, in late 1862, the general-in-chief whom he had been seeking: Ulysses S. Grant.

Throughout the war Lincoln sympathetically pardoned many Union soldiers who were guilty of breaches of military discipline, although he could be stern when necessary, such as when he refused to lift death sentences given to five bounty jumpers*. As the war drew to a successful conclusion, he said, at his second inauguration, that the South should not be blamed for the war and he urged his countrymen to leniency.

*Bounty jumpers were men who were paid by states, cities or counties for enlistment and deserted after collecting their bounties.

ATTENTION
VOLUNTEERS

WANTED!
ABLE-BODIED MEN TO FILL UP
COMPANY C,
131st REGIMENT PENN'A VOL.
UNDER COMMAND OF
COL. ELISHA W. DAVIS.

RECRUITING OFFICE:
N. W. Cor. of FOURTH & WALNUT STS.

CLOTHES AND RATIONS FURNISHED IMMEDIATELY
ON BEING MUSTERED IN.
CHAS. F. ROBERTSON, Capt.

I. M. BURROWS, 1st Lieut.   **W. W. WATT, 2nd Lieut.**

General William T. Sherman discusses Union peace terms with Lincoln in the presence of General Ulysses S. Grant and Admiral David D. Porter.

Trust your own judgement of public service . . .

Address on Colonization to a Deputation of Negroes, Aug. 14, 1862

. . . .Without the institution of slavery, and the colored race as a basis, the war could not have an existence.

Annual Message to Congress, Dec. 8, 1863

In the midst of other cares, however important, we must not lose sight of the fact that the war power is still our main reliance. To that power alone can we look yet for a time, to give confidence to the people in the contested regions that the insurgent power will not again overrun them. Until that confidence shall be established, little can be done anywhere for what is called reconstruction.

Letter to Major General George G. Meade, July 27, 1863

Do not lean a hair's breadth against your own feelings or your judgment of the public service on the idea of gratifying me.

Letter to Union Governors, July 3, 1862

The quicker you send [recruits for Army], the fewer you will have to send. *Time* is everything. Please act in view of this.

Letter to Major General David Hunter, Dec. 31, 1861

"Act well your part, there all the honor lies." He who does *something* at the head of a regiment will eclipse him who does *nothing* at the head of a hundred.

General George G. Meade defeated Confederate General, Robert E. Lee at Gettysburg, later site of Lincoln's historic address of 1863.

General William T. Sherman's tactics during the Battle of Shiloh and his capture of Savannah highlighted his Civil War career.

Letter to Major General Joseph Hooker, Jan. 26, 1863

Beware of rashness, but with energy and sleepless vigilance go forward and give us victories.

Letter [entire message] to Governor Andrew G. Curtin of Pennsylvania, April 8, 1861

I think the necessity of being ready increases. Look to it.

Letter to General William T. Sherman, Dec. 26, 1864

Many, many thanks for your Christmas gift, the capture of Savannah.

When you were about leaving Atlanta for the Atlantic coast I was *anxious* if not fearful; but feeling that you were the better judge and remembering that "nothing risked, nothing gained," I did not interfere. Now, the undertaking being a success, the honor is all yours; for I believe none of us went further than to acquiesce.

Annual Message to Congress, Dec. 6, 1864

. . . The war will cease on the part of the Government whenever it shall have ceased on the part of those who began it.

Lincoln's last wartime Union Army commander, General Ulysses S. Grant.

Lincoln's visit to a Union Army position at City Point, Virginia, is depicted in a lithograph from a painting by Gustav Bartsch.

Letter to Lieutenant General Ulysses S. Grant, April 30, 1864

Not expecting to see you again before the Spring campaign opens, I wish to express, in this way, my entire satisfaction with what you have done up to this time, so far as I understand it. The particulars of your plans I neither know or seek to know. You are vigilant and self-reliant; and, pleased with this, I wish not to obtrude any constraints or restraints upon you. While I am very anxious that any great disaster or the capture of our men in great numbers shall be avoided, I know these points are less likely to escape your attention than they would be mine. If there is anything wanting which is within my power to give, do not fail to let me know it.

And now with a brave Army, and a just cause, may God sustain you.

Order for Sabbath Observance, Nov. 15, 1862

The President . . . desires and enjoins the orderly observance of the Sabbath by the officers and men in the military and naval service. The importance for man and beast of the prescribed weekly rest, the sacred rights of Christian soldiers and sailors, a becoming deference to the best sentiment of a Christian people, and a due regard for the Divine will demand that Sunday labor in the army and navy be reduced to the measure of strict necessity.

Response to a Serenade, Nov. 10, 1864

We cannot have free government without elections; and if the rebellion could force us to forego or postpone a national election, it might fairly claim to have already conquered and ruined us. The strife of the election is but human nature practically applied to the facts of the case. What has occurred in this case [1864 election] must ever recur in similar cases. Human nature will not change. In any future great national trial, compared with the men of this, we shall have weak and as strong, as silly and as wise, as bad and good. Let us, therefore, study the incidents of this as philosophy to learn wisdom from, and none of them as wrongs to be revenged.

Proclamation Concerning Reconstruction, July 8, 1864

I am . . . unprepared . . . to be inflexibly committed to any single plan of restoration, and while I am also unprepared to declare that the free state constitutions and governments already adopted and installed in Arkansas and Louisiana shall be set aside and held for naught, thereby repelling and discouraging the loyal citizens who have set up the same as to further effort, or to declare a constitutional competency in Congress to abolish slavery in states, but I am at the same time sincerely hoping and expecting that a constitutional amendment abolishing slavery throughout the nation may be adopted. . . .

Freelance Photographers Guild photo by Thomas Jonathan

Confederate General Thomas J. Jackson's daring maneuvers at Manassas Junction, Virginia, earned him the name "Stonewall."

If there is anything wanting that is within my power to give, do not fail to let me know . . .

Lincoln met General George B. McClellan, facing the President in the foreground, at Antietam, Maryland, in October, 1862.

Bettmann Archive

In this sad world

sorrow comes to all

but we have saved

the Union . . .

The sounds of war were distant echos as Lincoln's son Thomas (Tad)
posed in a Union Army colonel's uniform.

A company of Union soldiers stand inspection in unusual uniforms
adopted from the French Zouaves who fought in the Civil War.

The war destroyed men and machines with equal vengeance.
Railroad damage at Manassas Junction, Virginia, in March, 1862.

The face of death is revealed in a photograph of war dead
after the Battle of Gettysburg in 1864.

Colonel Elmer E. Ellsworth, the first Union officer killed in the war. Lincoln wrote Ellsworth's parents a moving letter of condolence.

suddenly dashed, as in his fall. In size, in years, and in youthful appearance, a boy only, his power to command men, was surpassingly great. This power, combined with a fine intellect, an indomitable energy, and a taste altogether military, constituted in him, as seemed to me, the best natural talent in that department I ever knew. And yet he was singularly modest and deferential in social intercourse. My acquaintance with him began less than two years ago; yet through the latter half of the intervening period, it was as intimate as the disparity of our ages, and my engrossing engagements, would permit. To me, he appeared to have no indulgences or pastimes; and I never heard him utter a profane, or an intemperate word. What was conclusive of his good heart, he never forgot his parents. The honors he labored for so laudably, and, in the sad end, so gallantly gave his life, he meant for them, no less than for himself.

In the hope that it may be no intrusion upon the sacredness of your sorrow, I have ventured to address you this tribute to the memory of my young friend, and your brave and early fallen child.

May God give you that consolation which is beyond all earthly power. Sincerely your friend in a common affliction.

Letter to Fanny McCullough, Dec. 23, 1862

It is with deep grief that I learn of the death of your kind and brave father, and especially that it is affecting your young heart beyond what is common in such cases. In this sad world of ours, sorrow comes to all, and to the young it comes with bitterest agony because it takes them unawares. . . . Perfect relief is not possible, except with time. You cannot now realize that you will ever feel better. Is not this so? And yet it is a mistake. You are sure to be happy again. To know this, which is certainly true, will make you some less miserable now. I have had experience enough to know what I say, and you need only to believe it to feel better at once. The memory of your dear father, instead of an agony, will yet be a sad, sweet feeling in your heart, of a purer and holier sort than you have known before.

Letter to Ephraim D. and Phoebe Ellsworth, May 25, 1861

My dear Sir and Madam:

In the untimely loss of your noble son, our affliction here is scarcely less than your own. So much of promised usefulness to one's country, and of bright hopes for one's self and friends, have rarely been so

A contemporary bust of Lincoln, Leo Cherne.

Letter to Mrs. Lydia Bixby, Nov. 21, 1864

Dear Madam:

I have been shown in the files of the War Department a statement of the Adjutant General of Massachusetts that you are the mother of five sons who have died gloriously on the field of battle. I feel how weak and fruitless must be any words of mine which should attempt to beguile you from the grief of a loss so overwhelming. But I cannot refrain from tendering to you the consolation that may be found in the thanks of the Republic they died to save.

I pray that our Heavenly Father may assuage the anguish of your bereavement, and leave you only the cherished memory of the loved and lost, and the solemn pride that must be yours to have laid so costly a sacrifice upon the altar of freedom.

Response to Methodists, May 18, 1864

It is no fault in others that the Methodist Church sends more soldiers to the field, more nurses to the hospital, and more prayers to heaven than any. God bless the Methodist Church. Bless all the churches, and blessed be God, Who, in this our great trial, giveth us the churches.

Address at Sanitary Fair, Baltimore, Maryland, April 18, 1864

When the war began three years ago neither party, nor any man, expected it would last till now. Each looked for the end, in some way, long ere today. Neither did any anticipate that domestic slavery would be much affected by the war. But here we are; the war has not ended, and slavery has been much affected—how much needs not now be recounted. So true it is that man proposes, and God disposes.

Letter to Thurlow Weed*, March 15, 1865

Men are not flattered by being shown that there has been a difference of purpose between the Almighty and them. To deny it, however, in this case, is to deny that there is a God governing the world. It is a truth which I thought needed to be told, and, as whatever of humiliation there is in it falls most directly on myself, I thought others might afford for me to tell it.

———————————————————

*Referring to second inaugural address.

Confederate earthworks on the heights of Centreville, Virginia, were built during the months following the Southern victory at the 1861 battle of Bull Run which occurred nearby.

Second Inaugural Address, Washington, D.C., March 4, 1865

Fellow-Countrymen: At this second appearing to take the oath of the Presidential office, there is less occasion for an extended address than there was at the first. Then, a statement, somewhat in detail, of a course to be pursued, seemed fitting and proper. Now, at the expiration of four years, during which public declarations have been constantly called forth on every point and phase of the great contest which still absorbs the attention and engrosses the energies of the nation, little that is new could be presented. The progress of our arms, upon which all else chiefly depends, is as well known to the public as to myself; and it is, I trust, reasonably satisfactory and encouraging to all. With high hope for the future, no prediction in regard to it is ventured.

On the occasion corresponding to this four years ago, all thoughts were anxiously directed to an impending civil war. All dreaded it—all sought to avert it. While the inaugural address was being delivered from this place, devoted altogether to *saving* the Union without war, insurgent agents were in the city seeking to *destroy* it without war—seeking to dissolve the Union, and divide effects, by negotiation. Both parties deprecated war; but one of them would *make* war rather than let the nation survive; and the other would *accept* war rather than let it perish. And the war came.

One-eighth of the whole population were colored slaves, not distributed generally over the Union, but localized in the southern part of it. These slaves constituted a peculiar and powerful interest. All knew that this interest was, somehow, the cause of the war. To strengthen, perpetuate and extend this interest

This monster mortar was used for a short time in 1864 in the siege in and around Petersburg, Virginia. Because it weighed 17,12 pounds it had to be transported by railway car.

was the object for which the insurgents would rend the Union, even by war; while the Government claimed no right to do more than to restrict the territorial enlargement of it. Neither party expected for the war the magnitude or the duration which it has already attained. Neither anticipated that the *cause* of the conflict might cease with, or even before, the conflict itself should cease. Each looked for an easier triumph and a result less fundamental and astounding. Both read the same Bible, and pray to the same God; and each invokes His aid against the other. It may seem strange that any men should dare to ask a just God's assistance in wringing their bread from the sweat of other men's faces; but let us judge not, that we be not judged. The prayers of both could not be answered— that of neither has been answered fully. The Almighty has His own purposes. "Woe unto the world because of offenses! for it must needs be that offenses come; but woe to that man by whom the offense cometh!" If we shall suppose that American slavery is one of those offenses which, in the providence of God, must needs come, but which, having continued through

His appointed time, He now wills to remove, and that He gives to both North and South this terrible war, as the woe due to those by whom the offense came, shall we discern therein any departure from those divine attributes which the believers in a living God always ascribe to Him? Fondly do we hope—fervently do we pray—that this mighty scourge of war may speedily pass away. Yet, if God wills that it continue until all the wealth piled by the bondman's 250 years of unrequited toil shall be sunk, and until every drop of blood drawn with the lash shall be paid by another drawn with the sword, as was said 3000 years ago, so still it must be said: "The judgments of the Lord are true and righteous altogether."

With malice toward none; with charity for all; with firmness in the right, as God gives us to see the right, let us strive on to finish the work we are in; to bind up the nation's wounds; to care for him who shall have borne the battle, and for his widow, and his orphan—to do all which may achieve and cherish a just and a lasting peace among ourselves, and with all nations.

An illustration in Harper's Weekly showing Lincoln making his Gettysburg Address.

It is for us, the living, rather to be dedicated here to the great task remaining before us . . .

Address Delivered at the Dedication of the Cemetery at Gettysburg, Nov. 19, 1863

Four score and seven years ago our fathers brought forth upon this continent a new nation, conceived in liberty, and dedicated to the proposition that all men are created equal.

Now we are engaged in a great civil war, testing whether that nation, or any nation so conceived and so dedicated, can long endure. We are met here on a great battlefield of that war. We have come to dedicate a portion of it as a final resting place for those who here gave their lives that that nation might live. It is altogether fitting and proper that we should do this.

But, in a larger sense, we cannot dedicate—we cannot consecrate—we cannot hallow this ground. The brave men, living and dead, who struggled here, have consecrated it far above our poor power to add or detract. The world will little note nor long remember what we say here, but can never forget what they did here. It is for us, the living, rather to be dedicated here to the unfinished work which they have, thus far, so nobly carried on. It is rather for us to be here dedicated to the great task remaining before us—that from these honored dead we take increased devotion to that cause for which they here gave the last full measure of devotion; that we here highly resolve that these dead shall not have died in vain; that this nation shall have a new birth of freedom; and that this Government of the people, by the people, for the people, shall not perish from the earth.

Letter to Willie Smith, Feb. 23, 1864

Your friend, Leroy C. Driggs, tells me you are a very earnest friend of mine, for which please allow me to thank you. You and those of your age [twelve] are to take charge of this country when we older ones shall have gone; and I am glad to learn that you already take so lively an interest in what just now so deeply concerns us.

Today the cannon at Gettysburg stand among quiet surroundings.

Frank Aleksandrowicz

With the possible exception of D-Day, 1944, probably no battle in American history has seared itself into the American memory as has the contest at Gettysburg, Pennsylvania, July, 1863. A related clash occurred at Wrightsville, about 40 miles from Gettysburg. In July, 1963 the centennial of that fight was marked by a re-created skirmish by men and boys in full blue and gray battle dress.

All photos on this page by Frank Aleksandrowicz

One of the cannons that contributed to
28,000 Southern dead, wounded and missing.

Left: Little Round Top, one of the
primary Union strongholds which
Confederate forces tried to capture
and failed. The Southern defeats at
Gettysburg and Vicksburg, Mississippi,
within a day of each other marked
the beginning of the end for the
Confederacy.

General Robert E. Lee surrenders to General Ulysses S. Grant in the
front parlor of McClean House at Appomattox Court House.

We here highly resolve that these dead shall not have died in vain,
that this nation shall have a new birth of freedom . . .

Overleaf: Lincoln's drive through Richmond, April 5, 1865.

In the midst of this, He from Whom all blessings flow must not be forgotten . . .

Last Public Address, Washington, D.C., April 11, 1865

We meet this evening, not in sorrow, but in gladness of heart. The evacuation of Petersburg and Richmond, and the surrender of the principal insurgent army, give hope of a righteous and speedy peace whose joyous expression can not be restrained. In the midst of this, however, He from Whom all blessings flow, must not be forgotten. A call for a national thanksgiving is being prepared, and will be duly promulgated. Nor must those whose harder part gives us the cause for rejoicing, be overlooked. Their honors must not be parcelled out with others. I myself was near the front, and had the high pleasure of transmitting much of the good news to you, but no part of the honor, for plan or execution, is mine. To General Grant, his skillful officers, and brave men, all belongs. The gallant Navy stood ready, but was not in reach to take active part.

By these recent successes the re-inauguration of the national authority—reconstruction—which has had a large share of thought from the first, is pressed much more closely upon our attention. It is fraught with great difficulty. Unlike the case of a war between independent nations, there is no authorized organ for us to treat with. No one man has authority to give up the rebellion for any other man. We simply must begin with, and mould from, disorganized and discordant elements. Nor is it a small additional embarrassment that we, the loyal people, differ among ourselves as to the mode, manner and means of reconstruction.

VII

LINCOLN, PERSONAL AND PRIVATE

MY CHILDHOOD-HOME I SEE AGAIN

My childhood-home I see again,
And gladden with the view;
And still as mem'ries crowd my brain,
There's sadness in it too.

O memory! thou mid-way world
'Twixt Earth and Paradise,
Where things decayed, and loved ones lost
In dreamy shadows rise. . . .

I range the fields with pensive tread,
And pace the hollow rooms;
And feel (companions of the dead)
I'm living in the tombs. . . .

Now fare thee well: more thou the cause
Than subject now of woe.
All mental pangs, but time's kind laws,
Hast lost the power to know.

And now away to seek some scene
Less painful than the last—
With less of horror mingled in
The present and the past.

The very spot where grew the bread
That formed my bones, I see.
How strange, old field, on thee to tread,
And feel I'm part of thee!

These lines are from a poem written by Lincoln not long after he visited his old home in Indiana while taking the stump for Henry Clay in 1844. Although he said that region was "as unpoetical as any spot on earth," it moved him deeply to see it again. The incident gives special insight into Lincoln, the man, the son, the husband, the father, the friend—the Lincoln that has come to be most loved.

Lincoln was a man of order and thrift, eating frugally, neither drinking nor smoking. There is ample evidence that he loved both his mother and step-mother, caring for the latter until his death. While President he was generous in appointing his old friends to office. In the White House Mrs. Lincoln's indiscretions born of good intentions, her financial irresponsibility and the increased frequency of her "nervous spells" made her the object of political smears and greatly increased his burden. It was a burden he patiently carried without complaint. Their own private happiness endured while at the same time his qualities of tolerance, forbearance and forgiveness were refined. As a father, Lincoln was indulgent and when his beloved son Willie died in 1862, perhaps the hardest blow Lincoln ever suffered, he turned to young Tad and found great comfort in this kindly, merry and lawless boy.

Throughout most of his life, periods of melancholy oppressed him and they became more pronounced as he grew older. At the same time he had an indestructible sense of humor. In meeting strangers and acquaintances in official Washington and during crises he seldom lost his steady, assured manner, but he would spend evenings in his office swapping yarns with friends, giving full play to his wit and humor. He once wrote his sometimes intractable Secretary of War, Stanton: "I personally wish Jacob R. Freese, of New Jersey, to be appointed a colonel of a colored regiment—and this regardless of whether he can tell the exact shade of Julius Caesar's hair."

Statue of young Abe Lincoln, New Salem, Illinois.

Bedroom of Lincoln cabin near Charleston, Illinois.

Letter to Isham Reavis, Nov. 5, 1855

I am from home too much of my time, for a young man to read law with me advantageously. If you are resolutely determined to make a lawyer of yourself, the thing is more than half done already. It is but a small matter whether you read *with* anybody or not. I did not read with anyone. Get the books, and read and study them till you understand them in their principal features; and that is the main thing. It is of no consequence to be in a large town while you are reading. I read at New Salem, which never had 300 people living in it. The *books*, and your *capacity* for understanding them, are just the same in all places.

Letter to Andrew McCallen, July 4, 1851

I have news from Ottawa that we *win* our Galatin & Saline County case. As the Dutch Justice said when he married folks, "Now vere ish my hundred tollars?"

From Autobiography* sent to J. W. Fell,
Dec. 20, 1859

There were some schools so-called [in Spencer County, Indiana, which became Lincoln's home in his eighth year], but no qualification was ever required of a teacher beyond "readin', writin' and cipherin' " to the rule of three. . . . There was absolutely nothing to excite ambition for education. Of course, when I came of age I did not know much. Still, somehow, I could read, write and cipher to the rule of three, but that was all. I have not been to school since. The little advance I now have upon this store of education, I have picked up from time to time under the pressure of necessity.

I was raised to farm work, which I continued till I was 22.

Speech, Cincinnati, Ohio, Sept. 17, 1859

. . . I have found that when one is embarrassed, usually the shortest way to get through with it is to quit talking or thinking about it, and go at something else.

*Lincoln wrote this autobiography after several months of urging by Mr. Fell, a friend and politician who believed that Lincoln's Presidential prospects would be enhanced if people outside of Illinois knew something of Lincoln's background. About it, Lincoln said: "There is not much of it, for the reason, I suppose, that there is not much of me." It was used as the basis for an article which was published extensively in newspapers.

Above: Lincoln once practiced law in this log cabin courthouse in Decatur, Illinois, which was built in 1829.

Below: Interior of the Lincoln cabin which was reconstructed during the 1930s south of Charleston, Illinois.

If you are resolutely determined to make a lawyer of yourself, the thing is more than half done already . . . Get the books and read and study them till you understand them in their principal features . . .

Chicago Historical Society

Lincoln, "The Railsplitter," by an unknown artist, about 1858.

Letter to Mary Todd Lincoln, April 16, 1848

In this troublesome world we are never quite satisfied. When you were here, I thought you hindered me some in attending to business, but now, having nothing but business—no variety—it has grown exceedingly tasteless to me. I hate to sit down and direct documents and I hate to stay in the old room by myself. . . . And you are entirely free from headache? That is good—good—considering it is the first spring you have been free from it since we were acquainted. I am afraid you will get so well, and fat, and young, as to be wanting to marry again.

Speech, Chicago, Illinois, July 10, 1858

It is said in one of the admonitions of the Lord, "As your Father in Heaven is perfect, be ye also perfect." The Savior, I suppose, did not expect that any human creature could be perfect as the Father in Heaven. . . . He set that up as a standard, and he who did most toward reaching that standard attained the highest degree of moral perfection.

Mathew Brady photograph of Mary Todd Lincoln.

Bettmann Archive

Letter to James H. Hackett, Nov. 2, 1863

I have endured a great deal of ridicule without much malice; and have received a great deal of kindness, not quite free from ridicule. I am used to it.

Letter to Secretary of War Edwin M. Stanton, July 14, 1864

. . . Truth is generally the best vindication against slander.

Letter to Secretary of State William H. Seward, June 30, 1862

. . . The loss of enemies does not compensate for the loss of friends.

From *Reminiscences of Abraham Lincoln,* by Joshua F. Speed

Take all of this book [the Bible] upon reason that you can, and the balance on faith, and you will live and die a happier and better man.

Address Before the Wisconsin State Agricultural Society, Milwaukee, Wisconsin, Sept. 30, 1859

To correct the evils, great and small, which spring from want of sympathy, and from positive enmity among *strangers,* as nations or as individuals, is one of the highest functions of civilization.

Reply to New York Workingmen's Democratic Republican Association, March 21, 1864

Let not him who is houseless pull down the house of another, but let him labor diligently and build one for himself, thus by example assuring that his own shall be safe from violence when built.

Fragment on Free Labor, Sept. 17, 1859?

There is no permanent class of hired laborers amongst us. Twenty-five years ago I was a hired laborer. The hired laborer of yesterday labors on his own account today, and will hire others to labor for him tomorrow.

Annual Message to Congress, Dec. 3, 1861

Labor is prior to, and independent of, capital. Capital is only the fruit of labor, and could never have existed if labor had not first existed. Labor is the superior of capital, and deserves much the higher consideration. Capital has its rights, which are as worthy of protection as any other rights.

Address Before the Wisconsin State Agricultural Society, Milwaukee, Wisconsin, Sept. 30, 1859

. . . No other human occupation opens so wide a field for the profitable and agreeable combination of labor with cultivated thought, as agriculture. I know of nothing so pleasant to the mind, as the discovery of anything which is at once *new* and *valuable* —nothing which so lightens and sweetens toil, as the hopeful pursuit of such discovery. And how vast, and how varied a field is agriculture, for such discovery. The mind, already trained to thought, in the country school, or higher school, cannot fail to find there an exhaustless source of profitable enjoyment. Every blade of grass is a study; and to produce two, where there was but one, is both a profit and a pleasure....

It is said an Eastern monarch once charged his wise men to invent him a sentence to be ever in view, and which should be true and appropriate in all times and situations. They presented him the words: "*And this, too, shall pass away.*" How much it expresses! How chastening in the hour of pride! How consoling in the depths of affliction! . . . And yet let us hope it is not *quite* true. Let us hope, rather, that by the best cultivation of the physical world beneath and around us, and the intellectual and moral world within us, we shall secure an individual, social and political prosperity and happiness, whose course shall be onward and upward, and which, while the earth endures, shall not pass away.

Letter to the King of Siam, Feb. 3, 1862

I appreciate most highly Your Majesty's tender of good offices in forwarding to this Government a stock from which a supply of elephants might be raised on our soil. This Government would not hesitate to avail itself of so generous an offer if the object were one which could be made practically useful in the present condition of the United States.

Our political jurisdiction, however, does not reach a latitude so low as to favor the multiplication of the elephant and steam on land as well as on water has been our best and most efficient agent of transportation in internal commerce.

Take all of the Bible upon reason that you can, and the balance on faith . . .

Reconstructed house in New Salem belonged to a prosperous businessman.

To my home, my friends

I owe everything.

Now I must leave

with a great task ahead . .

Commissioned to do a small painting of Lincoln,
artist John H. Brown had Lincoln's portrait taken in August, 1860.
Brown later wrote that Lincoln's hard facial lines
masked his true compassion.

Speech to the Springfield Scott Club, Springfield, Illinois,
Aug. 26, 1852

He [Edward Hannegan] was the son of an Irishman, with a bit of the brogue still lingering on his tongue; and with a very large share of that sprightliness and generous feeling which generally characterize Irishmen who have had anything of a fair chance in the world.

Second Lecture on Discoveries and Inventions,
Jacksonville, Illinois, Feb. 11, 1859

The precise period at which writing was invented is not known, but it certainly was as early as the time of Moses; from which we may safely infer that its inventors were very Old Fogies.

Letter to Henry L. Pierce and Others, April 6, 1859

All honor to Jefferson—to the man who, in the concrete pressure of a struggle for national independence by a single people, had the coolness, forecast and capacity to introduce into a merely revolutionary document an abstract truth, applicable to all men and all times, and so to embalm it there, that today, and in all coming days, it shall be a rebuke and a stumbling block to the very harbingers of reappearing tyranny and oppression.

Speech to the Springfield Scott Club, Springfield, Illinois,
Aug. 26, 1852

It soon came to light that the first thing ever urged in his [Franklin Pierce] favor as a candidate was his giving a strange boy a cent to buy candy with. . . . Forthwith also appears a biographical sketch of him, in which he is represented at the age of seventeen, to have spelled "but" for his father, who was unable to spell it for himself. By the way, I *do* wish Frank had not been present on that trying occasion. I have a great curiosity to know how "old dad" would have spelled that difficult word, if he had been left entirely to himself.

Proclamation of Thanksgiving, Oct. 3, 1863

The year that is drawing towards its close, has been filled with the blessings of fruitful fields and healthful skies. To these bounties, which are so constantly enjoyed that we are prone to forget the source from which they come, others have been added, which are of so extraordinary a nature, that they cannot fail to penetrate and soften even the heart which is habitually insensible to the ever watchful providence of Almighty God. In the midst of a civil war of unequalled magnitude and severity, which has sometimes seemed to foreign states to invite and to provoke their aggression, peace has been preserved with all nations, order has been maintained, the laws have been respected and obeyed, and harmony has prevailed everywhere except in the theatre of military conflict; while that theatre has been greatly contracted by the advancing armies and navies of the Union. Needful diversions of wealth and of strength from the fields of peaceful industry to the national defense, have not arrested the plough, the shuttle or the ship; the axe has enlarged the borders of our settlements, and the mines, as well of iron and coal as of the precious metals, have yielded even more abundantly than heretofore. Population has steadily increased, notwithstanding the waste that has been made in the camp, the siege and the battlefield; and the country, rejoicing in the consciousness of augmented strength and vigor, is permitted to expect continuance of years with large increase of freedom. No human counsel hath devised nor hath any mortal hand worked out these great things. They are the gracious gifts of the Most High God, who, while dealing with us in anger for our sins, hath nevertheless remembered mercy. It has seemed to me fit and proper that they should be solemnly, reverently and gratefully acknowledged as with one heart and one voice by the whole American people. I do therefore invite my fellow citizens in every part of the United States, and also those who are at sea and those who are sojourning in foreign lands, to set apart and observe the last Thursday of November next, as a day of Thanksgiving and Praise to our beneficent Father who dwelleth in the Heavens. . . .

Farewell Address, Springfield, Illinois, Feb. 11, 1861

No one, not in my situation, can appreciate my feeling of sadness at this parting. To this place, and the kindness of these people, I owe everything. Here I have lived a quarter of a century, and have passed from a young to an old man. Here my children have been born, and one is buried. I now leave, not knowing when, or whether ever, I may return, with a task before me greater than that which rested upon Washington. Without the assistance of that Divine Being, who ever attended him, I cannot succeed. With that assistance I cannot fail. Trusting in Him, who can go with me, and remain with you and be every where for good, let us confidently hope that all will yet be well.

Above:

Young Thomas (Tad) Lincoln often innocently interrupted his father's meetings to sit on his father's knee. Tad died when only eighteen years old.

Below:

Lincoln's first son, Robert Todd, was a lawyer and statesman. Secretary of war under two Presidents, he later became minister to Great Britain.

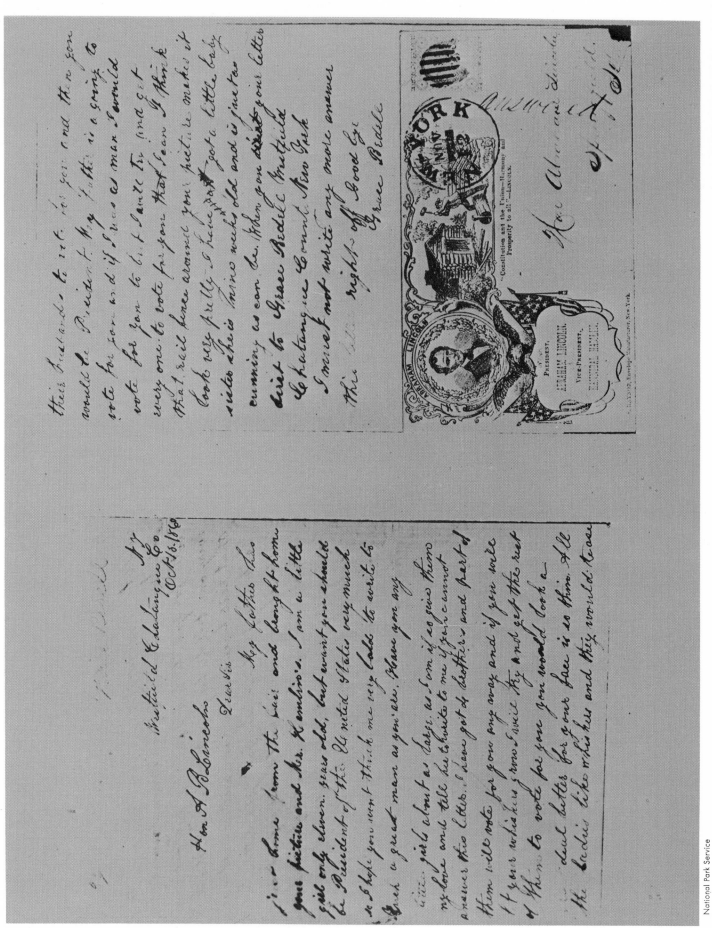

It is uncertain exactly why Lincoln grew a beard in the fall of 1860, but
one reason might have been this letter from a little girl, Grace Bedell.

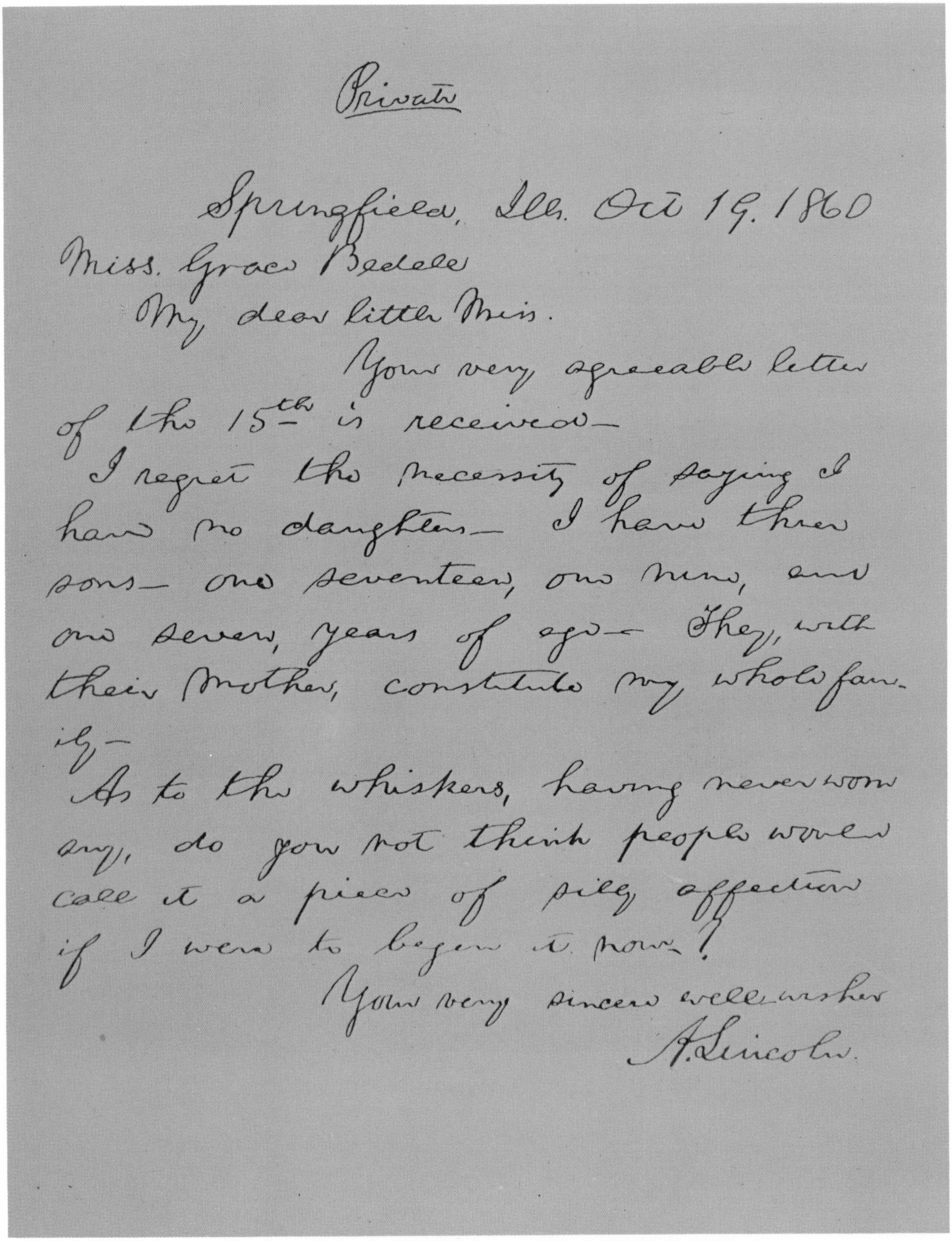

<u>Private</u>

Springfield, Ills. Oct 19. 1860

Miss. Grace Bedell

My dear little Miss.

Your very agreeable letter of the 15th is received—

I regret the necessity of saying I have no daughters— I have three sons— one seventeen, one nine, and one seven, years of age— They, with their Mother, constitute my whole family—

As to the whiskers, having never worn any, do you not think people would call it a piece of silly affectation if I were to begin it now?

Your very sincere well wisher

A. Lincoln.

Lincoln's reply to Miss Bedell demonstrates his wit and his love for children.
Within about a month after this letter, Lincoln began to let his beard grow.

The last photograph of Lincoln from life was taken by
Alexander Gardner in Washington, D.C., April 10, 1865.

Eulogy on Zachary Taylor, Chicago, Illinois, July 25, 1850

. . . His [Zachary Taylor] labor, his name, his
memory and example, are all that is left us—his
example, verifying the great truth, that "he that
humbleth himself, shall be exalted" teaching, that to
serve one's country with a singleness of purpose, gives
assurance of that country's gratitude, secures its best
honors, and makes "a dying bed, soft as downy
pillows are."

The death of the late President may not be without its use, in reminding us, that *we*, too, must die.
Death, abstractly considered, is the same with the
high as with the low; but practically, we are not so
much aroused to the contemplation of our own mortal
natures, by the fall of *many* undistinguished, as that
of *one* great and well known name. By the latter, we
are forced to muse, and ponder, sadly.

Lincoln's flag-draped Presidential box is shown in a view
of Ford's Theater as it appeared on April 14, 1865.

Lincoln was assassinated while viewing the play "Our American Cousin" at Ford's Theater.

Let not him who is houseless pull down the house of another, but let him labor diligently and build one for himself . . .

John Wilkes Booth assassinating Lincoln, April 14, 1865. Major H. R. Rathbone and his fiancée are at the Lincolns' right.

ASSASSINATION OF PRESIDENT LINCOLN, FORD'S THEATRE, WASHINGTON, APRIL 14. 1865.

The Lincoln Memorial, Washington, D.C., was dedicated in 1922.

EPILOGUE: A MAN FOR THE AGES

Good Friday, April 14, 1865, was a brilliant spring day. Lincoln rose early as usual and was in his office by about seven. During the morning he met with General Grant and the cabinet. Grant described his final drive of the war and gave details of General Lee's surrender five days before. Lincoln spoke kindly of Lee and other Confederate officers and said he hoped there would be no persecutions, "no bloody work," because enough blood had already been shed.

After lunch Lincoln signed a pardon for a deserter saying, "the boy can do us more good above ground than under ground," and he revoked the death sentence of a Confederate spy. By four in the afternoon Lincoln escaped from his office for a quiet drive with Mrs. Lincoln. He spoke of their life ahead: "We must *both* be more cheerful in the future—between the war and the loss of our darling Willie—we have both been very miserable."

Due to seeing visitors that evening the Lincolns finished dinner late. It was about 8:15 when they picked up Major H. R. Rathbone and his fiancée Clara at the home of Senator Ira Harris to take them to the theater to see Laura Keene in *Our American Cousin*. They arrived at Ford's Theater 15 minutes later, and the performance stopped as the Lincoln party entered its box. Lincoln acknowledged the cheers as he dropped into the haircloth rocking chair at the rear of the box. A guard assigned to protect the President sought a seat where he could watch the play.

In the third act Lincoln was enjoying the play immensely as Mrs. Lincoln reached out and took the hand of her husband. Then the audience below heard a muffled shot and a scream from the box; a man hurtled to the stage shouting something that sounded like "*Sic semper tyrannis*" ("Thus always to tyrants"), the motto of Virginia, and then hurried off stage dragging his left leg. The man was actor John Wilkes Booth.

Lincoln was carried across the street from the theater to the modest home of William Peterson, a tailor. Dawn brought a cold rain, and a silent crowd stood outside the home as rumors spread throughout Washington of plots against the lives of General Grant and Vice President Andrew Johnson. After holding on to life stubbornly for a few hours Lincoln died at 7:22 A.M.

Lincoln Memorial statue, Washington, D.C., was designed by Daniel Chester French.

Lincoln was assassinated at Ford's Theater
in Washington, D.C.
Originally a church, the building is now
a national historic site.

Lincoln was taken across the street
to the Peterson House after he was shot.

92

The reconstructed front and back parlors of the Peterson House where Lincoln died.

A light continuing in death's dark hour...

Lincoln's deathbed in the Peterson House where he died early in the morning, April 15, 1865.

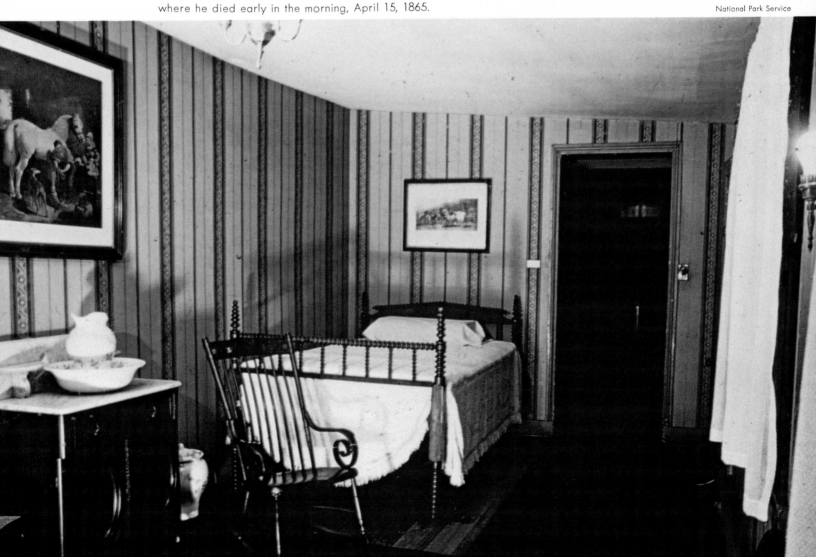

TRIBUTES

Now he belongs to the ages.   EDWIN M. STANTON, 1865

God reigns, and the Government in Washington still lives.

JAMES A. GARFIELD, 1865

Even he who now sleeps, has, by this event, been clothed with a new influence.
. . . Now his simple and weighty words will be gathered like those of Washington,
and your children, and your children's children, shall be taught to ponder the
simplicity and deep wisdom of utterances which, in their time, passed, in party
heat, as idle words.

REVEREND HENRY WARD BEECHER, 1865

A greater work is seldom performed by a single man. Generations yet unborn
will rise up and call him blessed.

REVEREND JAMES REED, 1865

[His] grave faults [were] over-leniency and generosity, deliberation and patience
—faults which would have been excellences in less desperate times, and which
even in these times have probably been our salvation.

REVEREND JOHN E. TODD, 1865

. . . In all America, there was, perhaps, not one man who less deserved to be the
victim of this revolution, than he who has just fallen.

THE LONDON TIMES, 1865

In President Lincoln we mourn a fellow citizen. There are no longer any countries shut up in narrow frontiers. Our country is everywhere where there are
neither masters nor slaves. . . .

ADDRESS BY STUDENTS IN PARIS, 1865

Abraham Lincoln . . . was at home and welcome with the humblest, and had
a spirit and a practical vein in the times of terror that commanded the admiration of the wisest. His heart was as great as the world, but there was no room
in it to hold the memory of a wrong.

RALPH WALDO EMERSON, 1876

If one would know the greatness of Lincoln one should listen to the stories which
are told about him in other parts of the world. I have been in wild places where
one hears the name of America uttered with such mystery as if it were some
heaven or hell. . . but I heard this only in connection with the name Lincoln.

LEO TOLSTOY (1828–1910)

THE CATAFALQUE, OR HEARSE,

AS SEEN IN THE FUNERAL PROCESSION OF PRESIDENT LINCOLN.

Published by H. H. Lloyd & Co., 21 John St., New York.

The Lincoln hearse and funeral procession, April, 1865.

But you have not told us a syllable about the greatest general and greatest ruler of the world. We want to know something about him. He was a hero. He spoke with a voice of thunder, he laughed like the sunrise and his deeds were strong as the rock and as sweet as the fragrance of roses. . . . He was so great that he even forgave the crimes of his greatest enemies and shook brotherly hands with those who had plotted against his life. His name was Lincoln and the country in which he lived is called America, which is so far away that if a youth should journey to reach it he would be an old man when he arrived. Tell us of that man.

TRIBAL CHIEF IN RUSSIA'S CAUCASUS REGION TO LEO TOLSTOY

95

Nowhere is the memory of Lincoln more revered than in Illinois. Several towns in the state, such as Dixon (where sculptures above and on opposite page are located), have a number of memorials.

From *WHEN LILACS LAST IN THE DOORYARD BLOOM'D*

When lilacs last in the dooryard bloom'd,
And the great star early droop'd in the western sky in the night,
I mourn'd, and yet shall mourn with ever-returning spring.

Ever-returning spring, trinity sure to me you bring,
Lilac blooming perennial and drooping star in the west,
And thought of him I love.

O powerful western fallen star!
O shades of night—O moody, tearful night!
O great star disappear'd—O the black murk that hides the star!
O cruel hands that hold me powerless—O helpless soul of me!
O harsh surrounding cloud that will not free my soul.

In the dooryard fronting an old farm-house near the white-wash'd palings,
Stands the lilac-bush tall-growing with heart-shaped leaves of rich green,
With many a pointed blossom rising delicate, with the perfume strong I love,
With every leaf a miracle—and from this bush in the dooryard,
With delicate-color'd blossoms and heart-shaped leaves of rich green,
A sprig with its flower I break. . . .

Coffin that passes through lanes and streets,
Through day and night with the great cloud darkening the land,
With the pomp of the inloop'd flags with the cities draped in black,
With the show of the States themselves as of crape-veil'd women standing,
With processions long and winding and the flambeaus of the night,
With the countless torches lit, with the silent sea of faces and the unbared heads,
With the waiting depot, the arriving coffin, and the sombre faces,
With dirges through the night, with the thousand voices rising strong and solemn,
With all the mournful voices of the dirges pour'd around the coffin,
The dim-lit churches and the shuddering organs—where amid these you journey,
With the tolling tolling bells' perpetual clang,
Here, coffin that slowly passes,
I give you my sprig of lilac. . . .

WALT WHITMAN (1819–1892)

ABRAHAM LINCOLN WALKS AT MIDNIGHT

(In Springfield, Illinois)
It is portentous, and a thing of state
That here at midnight, in our little town
A mourning figure walks, and will not rest,
Near the old court-house pacing up and down,

Or by his homestead, or in shadowed yards
He lingers where his children used to play,
Or through the market, on the well-worn stones
He stalks until the dawn-stars burn away.

A bronzed, lank man! His suit of ancient black,
A famous high top-hat and plain worn shawl
Make him the quaint great figure that men love,
The prairie-lawyer, master of us all.

He cannot sleep upon his hillside now.
He is among us:—as in times before!
And we who toss and lie awake for long
Breathe deep, and start, to see him pass the door.

His head is bowed. He thinks on men and kings.
Yes, when the sick world cries, how can he sleep?
Too many peasants fight, they know not why,
Too many homesteads in black terror weep.

The sins of all the war-lords burn his heart.
He sees the dreadnaughts scouring every main.
He carries on his shawl-wrapped shoulders now
The bitterness, the folly and the pain.

He cannot rest until a spirit-dawn
Shall come;—the shining hope of Europe free:
The league of sober folk, the Workers' Earth,
Bringing long peace to Cornland, Alp and Sea.

It breaks his heart that kings must murder still,
That all his hours of travail here for men
Seem yet in vain. And who will bring white peace
That he may sleep upon his hill again?

VACHEL LINDSAY (1879–1931)

This Dixon, Illinois monument commemorates the fact that Lincoln was stationed there as a Captain of Volunteers during the Blackhawk War.

Reprinted with permission of The Macmillan Co. from *Collected Poems* by Vachel Lindsay. Copyright 1914 by The Macmillan Co., renewed 1942 by Elizabeth C. Lindsay.

Lincoln Tomb, Springfield, Illinois.

APPENDIX

IMPORTANT DATES

Feb. 12, 1809	Born, Hardin County (now Larue), Kentucky.
1816	Family moved from Kentucky to Indiana.
March 1, 1830	Family moved from Indiana to central Illinois.
April-July 1832	Served in Illinois Militia.
Aug. 1832	Unsuccessful candidate for Illinois House of Representatives.
March 1, 1837	Admitted to the bar.
1834–1841	Served in Illinois Legislature.
Nov. 4, 1842	Married Mary Todd in Springfield, Illinois.
1847–1849	Sat in Congress as only Whig elected from Illinois.
Early 1855	Unsuccessful candidate for Whig nomination for Illinois Senate seat.
June 1856	Unsuccessful aspirant to the Republican Vice Presidential nomination.
May 18, 1860	Nominated on third ballot as the Republican Presidential candidate, Chicago, Illinois.
Nov. 6, 1860	Elected President with 1,866,452 popular votes to 1,376,957 for Stephen A. Douglas (Northern Democratic Party); 849,781 for John C. Breckinridge (Independent Democratic Party); 588,879 for John Bell (Constitutional Union Party). Lincoln won 180 electoral votes out of 303.
Feb. 1861	Plot to assassinate President-elect Lincoln at Baltimore, Maryland.
March 4, 1861	Inaugurated.
April 12, 1861	Confederates fired on Fort Sumter, South Carolina.
Sept. 22, 1862	Slaves proclaimed emancipated as of Jan. 1, 1863.

Nov. 19, 1863	Delivered Gettysburg Address.
June 7, 1864	Nominated on first ballot as Republican Presidential candidate, Baltimore, Maryland.
Nov. 8, 1864	Re-elected President over General George B. McClellan. Lincoln won 212 electoral votes out of 233.
April 14, 1865	Assassinated at Ford's Theatre, Washington, D.C.
April 15, 1865	Died at 7:22 A.M.
May 4, 1865	Buried in Oak Ridge Cemetery, Springfield, Illinois.

FAMILY

Father:	Thomas Lincoln (1778–1851). Born, Rockingham County, Virginia.
Occupation:	Farmer, carpenter, wheelwright.
Mother:	Nancy Hanks Lincoln (1784–1818). Born, Campbell County, Virginia. Married, 1806.
Father's Second Wife:	Sarah Bush Johnston Lincoln (1788–1869). Born, Hardin County, Kentucky. Married, 1819.
Wife:	Mary Todd Lincoln (1818–1882). Born, Lexington, Kentucky.
Children:	Robert Todd Lincoln (1843–1926). Robert Todd Lincoln was Secretary of War in the cabinets of President James A. Garfield (1881) and President Chester A. Arthur, who succeeded Garfield. In 1889 he became minister to Great Britain and served as president of the Pullman Company from 1897 to 1911. Edward Baker Lincoln (1846–1850). William Wallace Lincoln (1850–1862). Thomas (Tad) Lincoln (1853–1871). All the Lincoln children were born in Springfield, Illinois.